Praise for *Troubling the Water: The Urgent Work of Radical Belonging*

"An urgent, vibrant, and necessary call for justice, which is what God asks—demands—of us all."

—**Father James Martin, SJ,** author of *Jesus: A Pilgrimage* and other books

"*Troubling the Water* is a clarion call to walk toward the very people we see as adversaries. Doing the work of confronting implicit bias and bridging lines of difference with others can be grueling; in fragmented and unjust times, those things can be seen as complicit or even traitorous. But Ben McBride doesn't let us off the hook that easily. With engrossing stories, accessible theory, and strategies for everyday life, he schools all of us—whether we're powerful, privileged, persecuted, or prevented—in the strong language of justice, belonging, and even love. By reading this powerful book, you'll be poised to make the 'good trouble' to which John Lewis called us. This is a game-changer."

—**Jennifer L. Eberhardt, PhD,** author of *Biased: Uncovering the Hidden Prejudice That Shapes What We See, Think, and Do*

"This visionary and courageous book stands in the great tradition of Martin Luther King Jr. Ben McBride powerfully and persuasively shows how radical belonging and radical self-care are integral to a radical Christianity—a Christianity serious about the radical love of Jesus Christ."

—**Dr. Cornel West,** philosopher, activist, and Dietrich Bonhoeffer Chair at Union Theological Seminary

"At once practical and profound, Ben McBride's *Troubling the Water* reflects the hard-earned wisdom of the author—a practitioner and prophet. McBride's own story offers invaluable guidance for all who wish to be healing agents in our writhing world. But this is not a simple how-to book. McBride leads readers to the heart of the problem—we are failing to see each other (and ourselves) as human. Then he casts a vision and points the way toward a radical kind of belonging that challenges us all to the core. Read this book. It will change you."

—**Lisa Sharon Harper,** president of Freedom Road and author of *The Very Good Gospel* and *Fortune*

"Ben McBride is a bridge-builder. He is one of those rare leaders who can bring people together across the barriers that divide us, without compromising truth. He transcends the stale rhetoric, toxic self-righteousness, and paralyzing polemics of our day. I will continue to cherish every opportunity I get to collaborate with Ben and support his marvelous work. The world is a better place because Ben McBride is in it."

—**Shane Claiborne,** activist and author of *The Irresistible Revolution: Living as an Ordinary Radical* and other books

"*Troubling the Water* challenges us to find ways for everyone to belong across differences. This is a clear-eyed challenge to face into the real work of bridging divides and finding a way beyond 'us' and 'them.' Acknowledging where we have power and privilege and where we are persecuted and prevented allows us to create the path to the common good that is inclusive of all. Ben McBride is an engaging storyteller and challenges us to move forward together where all of us are agents of change and welcome."

—**Sister Simone Campbell, SSS,** attorney, author of *A Nun on the Bus*, and recipient of the Presidential Medal of Freedom

"Pastor Ben McBride is a national treasure. In his fierce, lifelong commitment to ending gun violence in America's most harmed communities, he's stepped up to the thankless, frustrating, but absolutely critical task of speaking truth to power in American policing. If we are ever to have the kind of policing that the Black and brown communities so long devasted by gun violence will see as legitimate, it will be because of the kind of engagement Ben McBride has modeled."

—**David Kennedy,** author of *Don't Shoot* and director
of the National Network for Safe Communities

"So often we talk about diversity, inclusion, equity, and belonging. Some of us have even developed a recipe for nurturing diversity, cultivating inclusive cultures, and assessing equity. Few, however, have embarked on an intentional journey to create a community of belonging. Through his deliberate lived experience on the front lines in Oakland, California, Rev. Ben McBride offers a compelling framework for addressing race-related violence and understanding America's social ills. As I turned the pages in McBride's master-class manifesto, I found myself no longer asking how I can make a difference, but questioning who I need to become if I'm to be a part of the solution. How can I wade into America's troubled waters? Enjoy this journey of self-discovery."

—**Cynthia Marshall,** CEO of the Dallas Mavericks

"Pastor Ben McBride is a true leader in every sense of the word. He embraces bridging at every level, including conceptually, spiritually, and practically. As the world struggles with fragmentation in search of a meaningful way to bridge, Pastor McBride may be one of our best hopes and greatest exemplars."

—**john powell,** director of the Othering and Belonging
Institute, University of California Berkeley

"Ben McBride is an exemplary leader—wise, courageous, articulate, and motivational. His character can, should, and does show itself in the wide spectrum of emotion and action necessary for a prophetic Black Christian man in America to have a voice of leadership and influence in the church and in the public square."

—**Mark Labberton,** president of Fuller Seminary

"There exists a mosaic of ideas that fuel transformative movements for justice. Yet while ideas about power, politics, and policy are important, Ben McBride shows us a critical missing element in our efforts to build a more just society: becoming. *Troubling the Water* is a brilliant and extraordinary glimpse into the inner workings of deep social change. Through profound insights from his years of work, McBride illustrates how our movements require deeper self-reflection about who we need to become to create the world we envision. Bold and tender, visionary and practical, fierce and precious, *Troubling the Water* is more than a great read; it is a moral and ethical compass pointing us in the direction of who we all need to become."

—**Shawn A. Ginwright, PhD,** author of *The Four Pivots* and Jerome T. Murphy endowed chair, Harvard Graduate School of Education

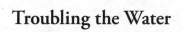

Troubling the Water

Troubling
the Water

THE URGENT WORK OF
RADICAL BELONGING

Ben McBride

Broadleaf Books
Minneapolis

TROUBLING THE WATER
The Urgent Work of Radical Belonging

Library of Congress Control Number 2023934432 (print)

Cover image: Shutterstock: Blue Texture
Cover design: Studio Gearbox

Print ISBN: 978-1-5064-8985-8
eBook ISBN: 978-1-5064-8986-5

Author's note: some names and identifying information
about some of the individuals in the book have
been changed to protect their privacy.

Printed in China

To Gynelle, who has loved me through my journey of becoming,
and to Brittani, Jasmin, and Symonne, for whom my heart beats

Contents

Introduction

There he was again. After a long and exhausting day of peacemaking and anti-violence work in Oakland, I arrived home to see him there, again. He, the brother, casually sitting on the front steps of my house, was uninvited and ready to verbally scuffle with me over whether he belonged there.

"Bro, come on, man," I pleaded wearily as I walked up to my front stoop. Early-winter darkness was gathering around us. "Can you get off my stairs? My wife and kids come up here." He didn't budge, and back and forth we went, debating over who had a right to take up this space.

I had these kinds of uncomfortable and sometimes tense interactions frequently, whether it was with someone sitting on my car, or playing loud music in front of my house, or chilling on my steps. My family and I had moved from a

San Francisco suburb to East Oakland in 2008 in order to be in close proximity to the community I served. "The Kill Zone," as it was known, was the locus of 70 percent of the city's annual homicides—a place where barbed wire, boarded-up shops, and slums are the results of decades-long racial divides, redlining, and the housing crisis. In 2012 alone, there were 131 homicides in the city of Oakland.

At the time, I was the executive director of Cityteam, a Christian nonprofit that provided opportunities—rescue and recovery, medical and financial, educational and spiritual—to hurting and unhoused Oakland residents. I worked directly with young adult men, ages eighteen to thirty, who were at risk of gun-violence involvement. My brother Pastor Michael McBride had also brought me in as a part of the Oakland Ceasefire Community Steering Committee. This committee—composed of representatives from the mayor's office, the police department, and the city's social services agencies, as well as a few community leaders—was tasked with steering the strategy to reduce violence in Oakland without using overpolicing methods. We met regularly to evaluate gun-violence data and trends and to create responses.

I often walked the streets of the city I had come to love. Block after block, from east to west, I'd pass makeshift pop-up memorials of balloons, teddy bears, and handmade signs with messages like "U will never B 4Gotten." Dollar Store prayer candles completed the displays. Some were often still burning from a recent vigil, and others had expired like the represented sons, fathers, brothers, sisters, and mothers who had perished. I'd pass by fellas who rocked "RIP" airbrushed T-shirts and hoodies like those popularized in the '90s as shout-outs to murdered hip-hop legends like Biggie and Tupac, a uniform of solidarity and respect. People used to wear black armbands to commemorate fallen heroes. Now those who mourned the dead wore the haunting face of the one they loved on their chest while hiding their broken hearts under their sleeves.

I mourned with those I didn't know and those I did—like Annie, a mother I met doing Oakland Ceasefire work. Annie had lost both her sons to gun violence within a seven-day period. The youngest, only thirteen, was killed in retaliation for the life his twenty-four-year-old brother had led. That life caught up with her firstborn and took him too. Annie lived with a grief that few of us know—a grief that leaves parents trapped in a constant state of bereavement shock, the living dead.

I knew the killings needed to stop. People needed to live, and the community needed to heal. As a minister, a peacemaker, and a leader within the anti-violence movement, I was there to make a change.

But this time, in this moment, on my front steps, I realized *I* was the one who had to change. I had to recognize that I was the outsider here. I wasn't born and raised in East Oakland. I had moved into *their* neighborhood, and I had brought along my privilege, my power, and my preconceived notions of how things should be. Some of the tension that existed between me and my loved ones in this community may have been them sensing my own mistrust and judgment of them.

So for some reason, that night, instead of pushing past the brother on the steps, I chose to pause, step back, and create space for a bridge—a bridge that would allow me to connect with this brother, witness his perspective, and understand his pain. As I stepped back and listened harder, something changed in the air between us.

After we had talked for a bit, he looked at his hands and then back up at me. "Man, no disrespect," he said. "But I grew up in this house. I used to live here."

His revelation, vulnerable and heartfelt, shifted something inside of me. Here we were, two Black men, colliding in this story together. He had a story long before I had arrived in East Oakland, just as I had a story long before I got there. He just wanted to chill on the steps of the house he sat on during his childhood. I just wanted a safe and clear path for my wife and kids to come and go. Forces that neither one of us created had put him outside of that house, and those forces had now put me—this new Black dude who ain't from around the way—inside it, telling him, "You don't belong here."

I learned over time that acknowledging and accepting his story—and the stories of all the folks I interacted with in the neighborhood—was necessary in order for us to get to a relationship. Hearing his story was a prerequisite for us to reach some level of understanding, to see each other in the most important way: human.

This example may seem simple. But it's through our daily interactions with each other and our willingness to create a bridge between ourselves and those we may see as our adversaries that we create space for radical belonging. That shift, I believe, is necessary not just when we get frustrated by our neighbors when we're coming home from work. It's necessary for our very survival on this planet.

Sawubona

I'm a Black man from San Francisco. I'm a father, a husband, brother, son, and more. I've ministered the Word of God because I believe it is a healing force and because my father did the same. I also carry generational pain. My parents grew up in the Jim Crow South, and my great-uncle was killed by the Ku Klux Klan (KKK). I care about helping people and addressing the issues that cause people pain, to the point of sometimes getting arrested for them (more on that later). I am that passionate. My size 13 shoes— whether Cole Hahn loafers, Timberland boots, or Air-Force 1 sneakers—lead me on a path toward justice, and that means I can be outspoken. But even though I go about being a warrior, I'm also vulnerable. All of this makes me walk a certain way. I also know that people are afraid of me, as a Black man, simply for being. That, too, makes me walk and talk in a very certain way. My walk and my shoes are my identity; they are my narrative. They are my story.

What's your story? How do you walk? How do you belong, and how do you create space for others to belong?

People sometimes think of belonging as the feeling of comfort when we are accepted, the sense of fitting in. But when belonging means simply acclimating to the status quo of the cultural majority, it stops being true belonging. Belonging can't just be the comfortable and happy feeling we might get as we nestle down with people who are just like us. If we think that, we have missed the point. Belonging cannot be held ransom for assimilation. Those in society who have long been considered the "other" hold valuable and honest truths. Their insights into life will always make us stronger, wiser, and more aware of areas where we fall short and how we can step it up.

That's where the *radical* part comes in. Radical belonging means cocreating with the "perceived other" to widen the circle of human concern. And what makes it truly radical is that it means doing this even when that very person or group seems to be working to constrict the circle of human concern. Radical belonging pushes us to imagine a world where the circle of human concern is big enough to include everyone—me on the front steps, the brother on the porch that used to be his. This includes those who are showing up to us as our enemies, and it includes even those who are manifesting a world that does not include us. This means expanding the circle beyond one that only includes us and the people who are marginalized—or privileged—like we are. It eliminates the widely accepted separation of "us" and "them" and elevates "we": collective humanity.

So for someone like me, who carries the trauma and pain of all unjust things that have happened to my family growing up in the South, radical belonging means imagining a world that can include an insurrectionist who proudly paraded through the US Capitol with a Confederate flag. In truth, I don't want to imagine a world that has room for that person. They can go to hell as far as I'm concerned. But if I am committed to radical belonging, this is the challenge I must accept. The man parading around the Capitol has to figure out a way to include me and other descendants of slavery in his vision of the future too. It's the challenge we all must accept if we are to snuff out othering, heal our planet, and save ourselves.

Sawubona is the Zulu greeting for "hello" and translates to "we see you." The response, *sikhona*, means "because you see me, I am here." The *sawubona* and *sikhona* greetings remind us that people aren't seen just because they are in a particular physical space; something must happen, collectively, for people to be seen. To truly see one another means being willing to bring people's lived experiences into ours. To truly see another—and to be seen—is an act of radical, reciprocal belonging. It's a greeting that suggests how urgent it is for us to see each other. It's almost like neither of us can exist apart from the other. Do I truly see you? Do you truly see me?

Whenever I encounter personal friction in embracing radical belonging, I remember a story that civil rights activist Andrew Young, a former US ambassador to the United Nations, told me about Dr. Martin Luther King. Ambassador Young, Dr. King, and a group of their comrades had stopped at the home of one of the sisters who prepared meals for them when they were on the road. It was a common practice in those times. During a discussion about white supremacy, Ambassador Young remembers, Dr. King reminded the group, "White people are no more inferior because of their racism than Black people are superior because of our ability to see their racism. We were both born into an unjust story." He continued, "What we've got to do is pursue our own liberation as a part of our own dignity, but we must do it in a way that doesn't cause us to actually become what we see in these white brothers and sisters."

Dr. King went on to say that liberation and belonging aren't one-dimensional. "As we get liberated, we liberate them as well," Ambassador Young remembers King saying, "as long as we pursue a world that has room for them to belong." For me, this story embodies the spirituality behind the civil rights movement, which aimed to get us to a beloved community. That spirituality asks us to recognize that even the "racist" children of God are children of God.

And that's where we are today: Our planet is sick, suffering from the ills of white supremacy and systemic racism. White supremacy is a global pandemic that is way more dangerous and deadly than COVID-19, the Spanish flu, polio, or any other disease. It has made the world so sick and has created fertile ground for othering: from policies to education to healthcare to finances and more. Because of the ways that people are being othered and oppressed here in the United States and around the world, we've entered a frightening time in our history when violence is becoming the first course of action for solving our disagreements or hanging on to perceived power. As a result, we're suffering more terror and chaos and unrest than we've experienced in generations, manifesting as the exponential growth of white nationalism, increased mass shootings, near coups of our government, and increased homicides within our communities.

Unfortunately, those on the receiving end of the cruelties of othering sometimes meet that violence with more violence. For generations, the message from dominant groups has been: "Because I don't see you as human, I am going to take away every ounce of your dignity and your ability to be human. I'm going to turn you into an animal and then ask you to rejoin society without treating the trauma caused by all of what I did to you." Those who are othered resist the oppression—often nonviolently, sometimes with tactical violence. But when the resistance strategies fail, the oppressed often become demoralized and choose violence too. This vicious cycle will continue until we collectively decide: "Enough." We have to get to a place where we all get to at least *exist*, even if we don't get along.

And to be clear: the world of radical belonging does not mean that I always have to be proximate to the folks who are showing up to me as enemies. The reality is that some people—because of the possibility of violence between us— might have to exist on different sides of the circle of human concern. But they are in the circle nonetheless.

The First Step

At this point, like the well-meaning person you are, you might be asking, "Okay, so what do I need to do to create a world where all can belong?" But I believe that's the wrong question. Each of us should be asking ourselves: "Who do I need to *become*?"

With this book, I offer a guide to help you answer that question, reflect on where you are, and begin your journey of building shared humanity, bridging across differences, and embracing radical belonging. I share my own journey as an activist and a community leader and reveal how dissecting and confronting my mistakes, my assumptions, and my own privilege along the way made me a better leader, a better human being, and a devoted champion of this belonging movement. And in these pages, I will also invite you to join the movement for radical belonging that our nation and world so desperately need.

I also ask all of you who have proximity to the levers of change to deeply reflect on who you are being, who you are becoming, and how you contribute to (or constrict) the space of radical belonging. Yes, those of us who are othered, marginalized, and subordinated can organize, we can protest, we can get all up in people's faces, and we can demand policy changes. And we should do those things. But those of you who have proximity to the levers of change need to be courageous, conscious, and committed disrupters as well. Now is not the time for you to stand along the shores. Now is the time for you to wade into these troubled waters. The ripple you create, no matter how small it may seem, could potentially transform lives and ultimately shift the world as we know it.

I get it. The decision to engage—to wade into the water—can be scary. Wading into the water of new situations takes some courage. There's an old Negro spiritual called "Wade in the Water" that enslaved Africans would often sing on their journey along the Underground Railroad in pursuit of freedom. One line says "God's gonna trouble the water," which is an image of healing and hope and liberation that comes from the Christian scripture. Wading into the waters is scary enough. But *troubling* the waters—the waters that other powerful people might tell you are calm and peaceful and don't need to be disturbed? That's even more difficult. When you trouble the waters, you might be told: "Stop making waves" or "Everything was fine before you came along and stirred up conflict!" Troubling the water requires you to see beneath the politeness and what Dr. Martin Luther King called "a false peace." That false peace is the absence of tension but not the presence of justice. Sometimes we need to stop keeping the peace and start disturbing it because the kind of peace that needs to be "kept" is usually the false kind. Sometimes we need to, as the great John Lewis said, "Get in good trouble."

Troubling the water isn't just a risk you're taking for yourself. Your child is going to have to buy into this. For white people, your whole family has to abandon white supremacy. For men, this also means abandoning patriarchy. For people of color who have access to power, privilege, and resources, this means being willing to sacrifice some things. We all have to be willing to take some risks. And you know what? It's going to be uncomfortable for a while. This work is hard. This work is messy. This work is sometimes thankless. But this work is necessary. I can't make it easy for white people, and I can't make it easy for anyone—including myself. But it is worth it.

I want to make sure we start with a common language that grounds us. So throughout the book, you'll notice I define terms that might not be familiar and give context for the way I am using them. Each chapter of the book is a particular call to action: to challenge your thinking, reflect on who you're being, and encourage your journey of becoming.

The Urgency of Now

As we take this journey together, I need you to understand the urgency of now. If we don't commit to manifesting a world of radical belonging—starting now—our world, as we know it, will continue to come undone right before our eyes.

If something does not change in the way we think about belonging in the United States—if something doesn't change about how we treat each other and who we treat each other as over the next twenty years—I think the country might fully come apart. By 2040, white folks will likely become the minority in this country, and we've already seen the fear and violent resistance to this. If there's not a mass movement to think about how we're going to show up differently, it's only going to get more violent. If you can't imagine a future that has room for those who feel like your enemies, it leaves room for the possibility of genocide. It also leaves room for the oppressed to actually become the very oppressors we are seeking to disempower. We set ourselves on the dangerous path toward violence feeling like a legit means to consider, depending on who's got the power.

Some of us are already making this frightening mental shift, believing that the country, and the world, would be better off if some people were just dead. One 2019 study that polled Republicans showed 15 percent of them said the country would be better off if most of the Democrats just died. Equally concerning was that about the same number—20 percent—of Democrats said the country would be better if a chunk of the Republicans just died. We are entering a moment when fear of the other is causing us to stop believing we are related and connected to each other across differences.

When violence that seems legitimate to masses of people begins to show up, it is way too late to start ringing the alarm bells. This is why I am making this plea now and why I am compelling you to do something. This is particularly true if you are among the Powerful and Privileged groups—which we'll talk about in chapter 1. I'm asking you to do something. Now.

If the country *does* come apart in twenty years, the people who are going to feel that the worst are Black people. History shows us that when things start breaking down in the United States, Black people are the canary of America's coal mine, and we're going to be the ones who experience it at a disproportionate level. As the saying goes, when white America gets the cold, Black people get the flu. We're 13 percent of the population, but we made up 30 percent of the COVID-19 deaths. In San Francisco, we are 3 percent of the city's population, but we make up 60 percent of the incarcerated people there. This is urgent. So yes, I'm seeking to safeguard Black people. But I believe this conversation about othering and belonging is urgent for the well-being of *all* of us.

We have seen enough of what othering can do. We have glimpsed the ways it could potentially end us. It's time for a new vision.

1

Understand Othering

As a man of faith, I try to see and value the humanity of others, no matter who they are. It is what I teach. It is how I live. It is what I believe. It is why I have committed my life to convincing the world that we need a spiritual revolution, one that reimagines our planet as a place with radical belonging at its center: where every one of us is brought into the circle of human concern, where we can be loved and accepted for who we are. I have faith that this world is possible.

But then I walk into an elevator with police officers and start sweating in fear. Or I'm shushed by a white receptionist as though I am a child rather than someone there to meet with her bosses. Or I'm denied a speaking engagement because my topic is "too Black." I—the man of faith, the

Christian, the human being who has every right to exist in this world—get othered daily, and I feel that heartbreaking experience deep within my soul.

Dr. john a. powell, law professor and head of the Othering and Belonging Institute at UC Berkeley, defines othering as "a set of common processes that engender marginality and persistent inequality across any of the full range of human differences." Violence, racism, sexism, homophobia, religious hatred, and intolerance all stem from this process of othering that many people cling to, whether consciously or subconsciously, in order to establish themselves as superior. After all, you can only feel superior if someone else is made to feel less than.

Othering is the greatest barrier to creating radical belonging in our world. It is a global phenomenon that occurs inside boardrooms, within communities, and across borders, and it has plagued us for centuries. This phenomenon has been used as a tool of oppression within our institutions for generations.

When I arrived in Oakland in 2008 to work with youth and launch the Oakland Ceasefire Community Steering Committee with my brother, Michael McBride, we knew that othering was our primary target. In Oakland, the police department has a deeply historical culture of othering that developed decades ago in response to the Great Migration. Between 1940 and 1970, in the second wave of the Great Migration, Oakland's Black population increased by more than 300,000, with folks escaping the racism and economic exclusion and terror of the Jim Crow South. There are more than 4,400 documented cases of Black people being lynched between 1877 and 1950. Often, white

Christian churches would dismiss early on a Sunday so that congregants could go watch the lynching of a Black person in the field. Bryan Stevenson's Equal Justice Initiative has created a powerful center for remembrance to pay homage to these victims. It was this brutal culture that many Black people fled, seeking a life free from white terrorism.

By the late 1960s, a grassroots organization called the Black Panther Party had formed in Oakland in response, with a core function of stopping police brutality against Black people by monitoring police activity—essentially, policing the police—and advocating self-defense. The Black Panther Party was eventually snuffed out, but othering at the hands of police had become deeply embedded in the community. It saw its crescendo in the 1990s with the Oakland Riders case, in which police were convicted of planting evidence on Black residents along with deploying unconstitutional acts of violence.

While we knew that these historical realities couldn't be changed, we determined that behavior could. When we began to focus specifically on eradicating othering within our work with the police and with young men from the community to reduce gun violence, we saw change. We shifted the way we related to the young men, and we helped them start changing the way they related to each other. We helped them understand the danger of othering—whatever form that took for them across difference—and we fostered in police officers a desire to stop othering the young men, in whatever form that meant for them.

As a result, we went four out of five years with no officer-involved killings—after the community had averaged six police-involved killings every year for twenty years. We reduced the level of nonfatal shootings between groups and individuals in Oakland from more than five hundred to fewer than three hundred between 2012 and 2018. Additionally, we saw a nearly 50 percent decline in homicides, with 2012 hitting a peak of 126 and dropping to sixty-eight by 2018. This work of building and bridging, and not othering or breaking, literally saved lives as we began to focus more and more on the work of belonging.

The Quadrants

When I speak to groups, I utilize my framework called the Quadrants to illustrate what othering looks like in our everyday lives. The Quadrants show how people make meaning of their identity and what it means to live within a larger story. Identity parameters for the four quadrants are what I call the 4Ps: the Powerful, the Privileged, the Persecuted, and the Prevented.

The Quadrants framework is a dynamic representative of our engagement with one another. It suggests that our tribal identity, where we live out our stories and connect with those who are most like us, exists within the back corners of the quadrant. (A quick note about terminology: In the context of this book, I use the word *tribal* to speak to the sense of connection we feel to the affinity groups through which our identities run. Our Indigenous brothers and sisters call on us not to use the word *tribe* or *tribal* in a negative context, which I greatly respect. As a descendant of Africans, I have love and affection for the word *tribe*; the sense of unity that it signifies comes from a place of high regard.)

When it comes to power, the Powerful often have the most, while the Prevented have the least. The Powerful are the people who get to say how things go. They can make a decision that impacts the conditions of those in the other three quadrants. They have resources to implement those decisions and the power to make sure they happen. The Powerful often inherit their conditions based on culture and history and structure. Let's look at an example. As the co-founder of an organization, Empower Initiative, I have the most power as the initial vision-setter and culture-creator. People were invited to expand the vision, bring clarity, and even challenge the direction, but because I co-founded the organization, I am historically positioned to yield or resist change.

The Privileged, while they might not be the people who get to say how things go, *benefit* from the status quo. Using the same organizational example, some colleagues had greater proximity to me when the founding of the organization occurred. I consciously and likely subconsciously developed cultures and structures with some of these people in mind, which meant they benefited from the status quo. Being proximate to me—being within my consciousness—during the design stage, they were advantaged. That wasn't their fault, but it still results in privilege.

Meanwhile, the Persecuted and the Prevented are often closest to the pain within our society. The Persecuted are restricted from experiencing full belonging even as they may sometimes get to experience the benefits of the status quo. But for reasons that are sometimes not obvious, the Persecuted are forced outside the circle of human concern. For example, in an organizational scenario, let's say a person who has experienced incarceration is included as a part of the staff. On the surface, they may appear to be a full team member, but they are not included in decision-making, perhaps because of preconceived notions on the part of the Powerful or Privileged about people with a record. The Persecuted often experience both access and restriction simultaneously because of various forms of difference.

The Prevented are those who, because of dynamics outside of their control, do not experience a sense of belonging in society at all. Realities regarding race, gender, class, religion, and immigrant status cause too many human beings to be left totally outside the circle of belonging. In an organizational scenario, the Prevented are those the Powerful and Privileged would never hire in the first place. This shows up in lots of ways: as Black, Indigenous, and People of Color (BIPOC) not being hired in the tech industry, for example, or not being allowed to live in neighborhoods with great schools and access to healthy food, or not receiving healthcare for addiction but instead increased criminalization. (Just look at the wildly different responses to the crack cocaine epidemic of the 1980s and the opioid epidemic of the 2010s.)

The idea of the Powerful, the Privileged, the Persecuted, and the Prevented shows up in various ways when we talk about the realities of race, gender, and class. Caste systems, as Isabel Wilkerson writes about so powerfully in *Caste: The Origins of Our Discontents*, relegate certain groups of people into the framework as we talk about it. When it comes to race in the United States, white people are the Powerful because of how power was taken violently and has been preserved over time. We can talk about how different groups in America have been—or currently are—Privileged or Persecuted or Prevented, and we can disagree about the particulars of that. But while we all get to have our own perspectives, we don't get to have our own versions of history. Data and social science research will always help us understand how different groups of people, at different points within this country's history, have benefited from the racial status quo, experienced both access and restriction, or been entirely prevented from the circle of human concern.

The fact that the location of any particular group in any particular quadrant is not entirely static can actually give us hope. It means we can change our story, any story, when we are willing to change the relationship among the Powerful, Privileged, Persecuted, and Prevented. We can work toward redefining what it means for us to belong.

It is incumbent on the Powerful and Privileged to become aware of how much space they take up in the quadrants and challenge themselves to be in relationship with the Prevented and Persecuted. And it is also important for the well-meaning Powerful and Privileged who want to help increase belonging to be aware of their obstruction spots. (Another terminology point here: *blind spots* is commonly used, but this term can alienate or other individuals who live with visual impairments; I've chosen to use *obstruction spots* instead.) As British author C. S. Lewis wrote in his novel *The Magician's Nephew*, "What you see and hear depends a good deal on where you are standing. It also depends on what sort of person you are." When you are the Powerful or the Privileged, you must listen to and truly hear—without defensiveness, without judgment—the

Persecuted and the Prevented. Otherwise, you may end up doing more harm than good.

One evening in 2013, I attended a public safety meeting in downtown Oakland. We were trying to engage with city council officials and get them to pass local policies that would give us some extended funding we needed for gun-violence reduction. This was always an uphill battle, and we received constant resistance and excuses for why it couldn't happen. Still, we waited. For hours and hours, we waited. I began to get irritated as other attendees in the mostly white crowd got up to talk about issues that didn't feel nearly as urgent as young Black men in this city dying of gun violence on the streets.

When a young white brother got up to express the need for bike lanes in the city of Oakland because of safety issues, my feeling was the same. Then something he said completely shifted my perspective. The cyclist told the city council:

Listen, when I'm riding the bike in Oakland, the person I am *not* concerned about is the loud, souped-up sports car that's barreling down the street. I can hear the noise of their engine. I can hear the screech of their tires as they're driving aggressively. I am always aware of them. I can feel them coming; I can spot them. I can keep myself safe. We need the bike lanes because of the soccer mom. The soccer mom has a good heart. She's likely driving the way one should drive, but she has so much happening inside her car while she is trying to get her child to their soccer game that she's likely to not see me in her blind spot when she makes that right turn. And she's the one who will hit me when I'm on my bike. She'll get out, and she'll nurse my wounds, and she'll care for me, and she'll call 911. But I need the bike lane not because of the sports car; I need the bike lane because of the soccer mom.

This story provides a profound analogy. It's the people who demonstrate the most overt expressions of othering and racism who often have our attention and focus. And yes, those are people we have to be concerned about; however, we can usually see those people coming. The racist, the misogynist, the homophobe, the loud one being nasty in their language: they're easy to pick out of the crowd. But sometimes we don't pay enough attention to people who are trying to do good in the world who are actually prone to cause harm. Because they have not yet become aware of the way that people are marginalized and impacted in society—for example, the Persecuted and the Prevented—they end up running over the very people they may have set out to help. They run over Black people; they run over women; they run over queer folks; they run over Muslims. Then, like the soccer mom, they get out of the car exclaiming, "Oh, I'm so sorry! I didn't see you."

This is my critique of many modern liberals as well. I have personally experienced a lot more harm from so-called "liberals" and "progressives" and their microaggressions (although nothing about them feels "micro") than I do from overtly racist conservatives. That harm comes from the pat on my back—from the "Hey, he's so smart and articulate," the sense of surprise, like I'm not supposed to be smart and well spoken. It's what occurs when a woman at the table says what needs to happen, and then all of a sudden, the white guy or the Black guy jumps over to "clarify" what she has already said. As if she needed approval for her words to matter.

It is possible the choices you're making today are actually contributing to violence and real harm. Whether you're a mother or a teacher or a minister or a millennial who marched the streets during the global pandemic calling for justice for Black lives, you don't get to align yourself and say "I am an ally" while at the same time raising your kids in predominately white spaces, ensuring the educational system that remains bent toward your children oppresses the Black and brown children. You don't get to stand in the pulpit and ignore the suffering of our LGBTQIA+ brothers and sisters right outside the church doors. You don't get to say we are in a relationship and that you are committed to creating belonging while privately working to maintain my subjugation.

I challenge any progressive or liberal who feels like they got this allyship thing down to recognize this: if you don't pay close attention to the work of belonging, you yourself can become a huge threat to marginalized people who are just trying to move through the world.

When it comes to the four quadrants of the Powerful, the Privileged, the Persecuted, and the Prevented, most of us live at the back corner of our respective quadrants, as far away as we can get from the others. It's where we might share racial identity, religious identity, or class identity. It's the place where we make meaning for ourselves in relation to other people. It's where we find our groups. As human beings, we are all tribal in nature. Since the dawn of *Homo sapiens*, we have found progress and survival by existing in packs. That's how we forged, that's how we protected each other, and that's how we developed communication.

But that tendency to stay among people just like us can become dangerous, particularly when instigated by social anxiety that prevents us from being the best versions of ourselves. Historically in the United States, whenever we have tried to expand the definition of the word *we*, fears and anxieties have pushed us to create a *smaller* circle of human concern instead of one that is wider. And as we feel those forces regulating us to a smaller circle of human concern, our tribalism is triggered, and ideologies push us to believe we are safer when we exist with people who are just like us, speak like us, love like us, pray like us, and live where we live. History has offered us a false choice. Choosing segregation from those who are different from us as a safety device is actually dangerous, not safe. The boundaries of safety keep shrinking, and we have now moved to the notion of political perspective—that if you don't share the same ideas I share, I am safer when I am segregated from you.

"Us" and "Them"

One of the things we have to look at is how we are defining the word *we*. I had the pleasure of joining a conversation in 2019 at the Sunnylands Ranch in Southern California with civil rights activist Robert "Bob" Moses. Moses was a leader of Mississippi's Student Nonviolent Coordinating Committee (SNCC), an organization that played a crucial role in the 1960s civil rights movement—which I sometimes call the *belonging movement* of the '50s and '60s. He worked heavily in voter education and registration in Mississippi. Other activists in this cross-generational conversation were Andrew Young, Janet Moses, Minnijean Brown, and some emerging activist leaders around racial and climate justice. We were twenty elders and twenty younger leaders gathered in a room.

We'd gone very late into the evening when Brother Bob began to quote the preamble to the Constitution of the United States. We'd been listening to Sweet Honey in the Rock's "Ella's Song" by Bernice Johnson Reagon, with its pulsing rhythm and momentous lyrics: "We who believe in freedom cannot rest." Sitting in a large circle, we sat silently as this sacred music played over us. Then, as the song came to an end, Brother Bob faded down the music and began reciting the preamble. "We the people of the United States," he said. Janet Moses, his wife and renowned civil rights leader in her own right, began to recite it. Ambassador Young, sitting in his wheelchair, closed his eyes and began to recite it. Joan Baez, with a big grin, joined in. As they ended, Brother Bob repeated, with emphasis, "We the people. We the people!" He explained that all the work he has done—and that I do and you will do—is to expand the definition of the word *we* so that more people are included. It was like he'd preached an entire sermon in just three words.

Somehow, instead of expanding the definition of *we*, humankind has constrained it. Othering is the mechanism used to do so. We have massively devalued the word *we* in the way that we relate to each other as human beings and how we relate to one another in the context of community.

As a result, it is becoming our collective nature to perpetuate an "us versus them" framework.

I witnessed the "us versus them" framework in real time during one of my peacemaking journeys to Israel-Palestine in 2017. I was with a group by the Damascus Gate. We were standing in silence and in solidarity to mourn the death of a fifteen-year-old Palestinian girl who was killed by the army just the day before. She supposedly came at them with a knife, and they fired twenty bullets at her and shot her dead.

When we visited the Damascus Gate, which has amphitheater seating, the two other Black men on the trip and I never took a seat. We paced by ourselves, walking around the area. It was like we felt emotionally drawn to stand as we held space for the young woman who had been killed.

We were all at three different parts of the amphitheater when I noticed there were Israeli soldiers standing at the door. People were at first flowing through the gate without incident—until a brown-skinned Palestinian man walked in, that is. The soldiers immediately pulled him to the side and put him up against the wall. He got racially profiled for being. Just being. Immediately, I empathized with this brother and his experience in that moment. It was very familiar to me as a Black man in the United States.

The two other Black men witnessed the incident as well. While holding vigil for the girl, we each, in our silence, witnessed this darker-skinned Palestinian brother essentially being stopped and frisked. As he was being detained, I recognized the frustration, shame, and rage of being stopped simply because you are being othered. That day as we remembered the loss of a girl's life, I watched the way that, again and again, white supremacy and othering have a hold on us.

There were some tourists sitting around the amphitheater as if nothing had happened. People were taking pictures of the gate. Israelis (some armed with AR-15 rifles slung over their back) and unarmed Palestinians were going in and out of the gate. But the two other Black men and I remained on the perimeter.

When we all returned to the main group, I mentioned the incident to the others. Both brothers nodded their heads, signaling they witnessed it and were moved by it as I was. When I asked the fifteen white folks in our group, "Did any of you all see that?" their answer was no. None of the white people saw it. They were all there, but none of them saw it. But the three Black men, who were at three different locations—not with each other and not communicating with each other at the time—had all seen this happen. We had seen it, and we felt it, and we knew it, deeply.

This showed me two things: (1) the global impact of white supremacy and the way in which it has put darker-skinned people outside the circle of human concern all across the world and (2) how much those of us who have been impacted by that oppression see it instinctively. We see it. We feel it. Yet other people—white folks in particular and all who are in the Powerful and the Privileged groups of the Quadrants—have been conditioned *not* to see it. Even though we are living in the same world, we are in two very different worlds. So I and others who are among the Persecuted and the Prevented in these circumstances have to spend our time proving that what we see, what we feel, and what we experience is real.

Belonging work is so critical because if we are not careful, the white supremacy circle—the one that feeds the Powerful and the Privileged in the larger society—will expand. This will lead to more pain and more marginalization for folks who deserve relief.

Over the last twenty years of my peacemaking journey, I've found that our differences do not destroy the opportunity to build and expand the version of what it means to be "we." Our differences serve as fuel for us to find new ways to solve the problems that we all face. When we can find ways to come together across our differences and use the brilliance of our differences, we can create new outcomes that we would not be able to discover on our own.

You will discover this too.

What about "We"?

In 2018, the deadliest and most destructive wildfire in California history, named the Camp Fire for its origin in Camp Creek Road, raged out of control in Northern California. For years, the Indigenous people of that region had been telling the so-called "well-informed" officials that they needed to burn back and trim the forestry to protect the community and the environment from the dangers of an impending fire. But because of capitalistic interests and greed, people did not want to listen to Indigenous wisdom, which had existed for ten thousand years and had been passed down from generation to generation. The Indigenous people of the region had learned how to behave in relationship to the forest to prevent fires. They had learned to respect and honor the fire, to see it as sacred rather than something to be controlled. By not listening to that Indigenous wisdom, we had a fire that literally burned down acres upon acres of land, and homes, and cars, and picture frames, and photos, and memories: They all burned in that fire and lifted as ash into the sky. The wind carried that ash and that smoke all the way down into the Bay Area, where I live, and we were all breathing in those toxic fumes. We breathed in people's pictures, we breathed in people's memories, we breathed in people's cars, and we breathed in people's homes.

All because "we" did not include all of us.

We have not listened to a lot of the Indigenous wisdom that helps us think about how we should build society. We've had fires throughout human history, fires that have caused us to breathe in the smoke of burnt-up human experience, and they have choked many of us. No matter how much we aspire for belonging, we are choking, all of us, on the toxicity of the moment. We are choking on the mistrust that we have for each other across difference, we are choking on hatred, and we are choking on othering, and none of us is safe from it. It is something we're all breathing in, something that requires us not to just do something different but to *become* someone different, as individuals and as a people.

When people only focus on *doing* something different rather than *becoming* someone different, we experience human travesties. We see horrors such as the Indigenous genocide that founded the United States, the enslavement of Africans, the police shootings of unarmed folks in the back, and a host of other tragedies. When we don't stay on a constant journey of becoming, we may become enthralled by new projects and bold initiatives and other things that just reinvent the harm of history rather than actually repair it. Becoming is about challenging the ways we think and feel; instead of judging our thoughts, we get on the road to changing them.

As a result, those of us who are othered are constantly shifting, whether we want to or not. We shift in search of a place where we belong. The othering I experience in my life day to day is the result of what it means for white America to see Blacks. I can't not see race, and I can't unsee race. I am constantly breaking down white structure: a white way of being in this country that is deeply rooted in a power dynamic that wants to hold on to the status quo. Sometimes, to be seen and heard, I have to shift myself into more of a "white frame" to talk about what it is we need to do with each other. If I don't, blue eyes gloss over, and I'm tuned out.

Sometimes I make that shift on purpose because I don't want to always live within the race frame either. I don't want everything to be about race, so I try to accommodate myself to the colorless, comfortable world that white people tend to see. The world many white people are born into is one in which "color doesn't matter." Except then I wake up in the real world. I wake up protesting in Ferguson in 2014 because Michael Brown has been shot. I wake up marching in 2016 because Alton Sterling has been shot. I wake up crying several times in 2020 over a Black man in Georgia being hunted down and shot while jogging in his own neighborhood, a Black man murdered by a police officer on the streets of Minnesota as the world watches, a Black woman shot six times and killed by police in her own home. These realities are not something that I or any Black person can shape-shift our way out of. They are ever-present, which is why addressing them is urgent.

In This Together

I have spent a lot of years working across the differences of race, across class, across religion, across political orientation, and more. What these differences have taught me is that the more we anchor ourselves in our own factions—those spaces where we learned safety—the less we are able to access the deep interconnectedness that is available to us.

This book and this journey will help us reflect upon where we are in this moment of heightened tribalism and examine the type of changes we need to make as individuals, as communities, within organizations, and in society. How can we create a new story that begins to direct where we go as a people?

We know the "us versus them" framework is tired. It's worn out. Its energy only draws people back into their corners. We need a new frame, a frame that invites people into a sense of what it means for everyone to belong across difference. That new frame includes radical belonging.

In my call to foster a world of radical belonging, I'm not expecting people to stop being who they are as individuals or to abandon their groups. I'm inviting us all to become newer versions of who we are, deeper versions of who we are. Rather than only living life in the back corner of the quadrant, you can live at the intersection point, where our worldview—the way we are making meaning of our collective experience—is influenced by the way others are making meaning of their collective experience. My hope is that those of us who occupy that space in the middle will work together to widen the circle of human concern.

But how do we get there? How do we get to something new? One of the challenges we face when creating a new society and expanding the definition of *we* is that we've all been formed in the world as it is. Yes, we're all yearning for the world as it should be, but we may not know what that looks like. Like I said, we need to stop asking "What should I *do*?" and start asking "Who do I need to become?" We can also ask how *becoming* ultimately informs a new way of doing—one that is currently out of our collective reach. Who might we become in a world not as it is but as it should be?

2

Embrace Belonging

I was fired from my first pastoral job and then from my second. Those firings, while devastating at the time, led to some of the greatest lessons about the journey of becoming that I have ever experienced.

My first full-time pastoral job was in 2001 at one of the fastest-growing Black churches in the Bay Area. I was just twenty-four years old, and I had a lot of optimism about what that opportunity could mean and aspirations for what it could lead to in the future.

When I was about five months into the role, one of the other young ministers on staff came to my office and looked like he had just seen a ghost. He said, "I need to talk to you. Can we go to the basement of the administration building?" I said okay and went down there with him.

When we were in what he considered a safe space, he confided in me. Through tears, my colleague, who was twenty-three and a minister in training himself, shared that the head pastor of the church—our supervisor—had invited him to his house, tried to get him to watch pornography, removed his clothing in front of him, touched him in a way that made him feel uncomfortable, and attempted to seduce him without his consent. When the pastor told him he was going to take a shower, the young man ran out of the house, jumped in his car, and sped away.

I froze. I didn't know how to respond after hearing this news. As it happens when we are confronted with a difficult truth, I suddenly faced the formative question: Who am I going to become?

I thought about the fact that, to me, this pastor represented my future ability to become a successful Black pastor and leader myself. In some ways, he was holding the keys to my own vocational success. On the other hand, here was a young man who was literally crying out and asking me, as someone who was also in a position of power at the church, for help. He was being exploited.

My response to him was: "How do I know this is true?" I confess that part of me didn't want to believe it. The other part needed more time to think it all through and process what I was hearing. He responded, "I'm going to tell all the other people to whom this happened to come talk to you."

Over the next month, I was flooded with the stories of nearly a dozen young Black men, many of them college students. They came to me and said the pastor had done similar things to them too. When I sat with those brothers,

I asked them, "What do you want me to do?" and they would tell me, "I don't know what you're supposed to do. I just don't want this to happen to anybody else." But in their response, I felt like they were telling me exactly what they needed. They needed me to stand up. They needed me to leverage my power and privilege to speak up for them. They were the Prevented.

Now I had confirmation of the abuse—more than enough confirmation. And I stood at a decision point: Who was I going to choose to become in this moment of crisis? Was I going to stay on the shore and stay silent? Or was I going to trouble the water in the hopes that future abuse could be prevented?

I consulted close colleagues, who warned me that getting involved could be the end of my career or future opportunities. Ultimately, I decided that somebody had to confront the person who held the most power in this situation and who was grossly abusing that power. I held on to the belief that if I confront this and do what's right, good things will happen. Because if you do what's right, good things happen. Right?

So I confronted the pastor. Not only did I get fired immediately; he threatened me and vowed to block me from future ministry. "You'll never preach. You'll never do anything again. I'm going to destroy your name," he said. It was bad. And to make matters worse, all my colleagues, the other young ministers, turned their backs on me as well. Everybody was scared they might lose potential opportunities too.

For a long time, I questioned whether doing the right thing in the face of that kind of challenge was worth it. I lost a lot in the wake of that decision: my job, my career as a pastor, even my car. My oldest daughter was just one at the time, and my wife and I struggled to make ends meet.

A few years later, the scandal began to leak out, and more people learned about the pastor's abusive and foul behavior. Eventually, many of the people who didn't support me at that time came back and apologized. "You had the courage to do what needed to be done at that moment that we just didn't have," they told me. The experience remained formative for me because it occurred at the beginning of my ministry and forced me to wrestle with the notion of who I was going to become. Would I be willing to confront the underside of these kinds of dynamics and throw in my lot with the Prevented? Or would I be quiet in order to get future opportunities?

The pain of feeling betrayed by those I trusted in that situation has left me, but a lesson has stayed. That lesson was this: In order to create the world that I want to live in, I had to be ready to sacrifice—and sacrifice wasn't always going to immediately generate benefit. If I was going to contend for justice, fairness, and what's right, a cost would be exacted.

This is what we all have to understand when it comes to doing the work of belonging. There's a cost that comes along with standing up against those who have the power, and it may not always turn out well for you, at least in the beginning. That's the risk we have to be willing to take.

It is as Dr. King said about the Good Samaritan. Two people walked by the man on the side of the road and said, "If I stop to help this man, what will happen to me?" Dr. King said that's the wrong question. That was the question

I asked myself initially when the young minister came to me with his story of abuse: What would happen to *me*? But as I eventually learned, and as Dr. King reminded us, the Samaritan asked the correct question: "If I do not stop to help this man, what will happen to him?"

Refuse to Shrink

My second full-time pastoral position was at a large multi-cultural church in the center of Oakland. The church was started in the late 1960s by a white woman who had traveled from Canada to East Oakland to facilitate racial reconciliation and spiritual awakening with people across difference. Her vision was radical. At the time, the Black Panther Party movement was in full effect. To have a church led by a white woman that had Black and white folks worshipping together was rare.

In 2004, when I joined as a pastor, the church demographics were 50 percent lower-middle class and 50 percent upper-middle class. Forty percent were white folks, 40 percent were Black, and about 20 percent were split between Latino and Asian American people. I worked primarily with the young adults in the eighteen- to thirty-five-year-old range, which was the heart of the congregation. We were the melting pot of Oakland.

Our congregation was a staggering size, about three thousand members, and the building was a sprawling thirty thousand square feet. To serve our members, we had thirty staff members, a multimillion-dollar budget, and a variety of programs. We were well positioned to make a significant impact in the community.

At the end of 2006, Oakland, the community we served, was slated to close the year with 148 murders. This meant one person was killed about every two days that year. The city was unofficially segregated by the 580 Freeway, thereby creating East Oakland, which was primarily populated by lower-income Black and Latino folks, and central Oakland, which was predominantly white. One hundred and forty-seven of those murders happened on one side of the freeway in East Oakland, and only one murder happened on the other. There were also five hundred shootings citywide, meaning that, essentially, two people were shot every day, with at least two of those people dying every week in a city of 400,000 people. It was obvious that the community was in crisis.

One Sunday morning in church, I was singing and praising God with our diverse group of parishioners. We'd been praying dutifully for all the souls killed. Those 148 murders were heavy on my mind right at the moment that the pastor stopped the music and said, in a very well-meaning way, "Let's just stretch our hands toward the east, and let's pray that God stops the violence."

We all obeyed. We stretched our hands toward the east. We prayed that God would stop the violence. And then the music cued back up, and we kept singing our worship song.

But I couldn't sing. The song and the people in the pews around me suddenly receded. I paused and thought to myself, *There has to be something more that God is asking me to do beyond just stretching my hands toward East Oakland.* Praying and stretching from the safety of our church: it was way too convenient for me, and it was not responsive to the reality of what was happening in the city. Because if it were that easy to stop the violence, then why hadn't the violence already stopped?

The blood of Black and brown young men was drenching the concrete of Oakland, and no one seemed to be doing anything about it. My spirit was troubled with the pain of these deaths; how could this keep happening? If they were killing one another, how could these brothers and sisters here in the sanctuary not feel the value of life as I did? Why was there nothing in place to protect them? Why didn't anyone care enough to make it stop? Why didn't *I*?

I knew I needed to do something. So after that day, I began asking more questions during our church staff meetings. "How is it that we can raise millions of dollars every year, sending at least a third of our money overseas, yet not be responsive to the blood that's washing the concrete in our city?" I'd ask. "How is it that we can have eyes to see our global neighbors, who we think need to hear about our religion, and yet we don't see the young men who have grown up in our communities, who have played in our parks, who have gone to our schools, who even come into this very building?"

Those questions were met with swift encouragement to exit stage left. Soon the head pastor, who was also my mentor, invited me out for Chinese food. He was in his sixties and the son of the Canadian woman who started the church. He had been with the church nearly forty years. The only other full-time Black pastor on staff joined us as well. My daughter was sick at the time, and so we talked about her health for a while. Then the conversation suddenly pivoted, and the meeting became rigid and tense.

Maybe I should go do ministry with my brother, Michael, instead, one of them suggested. At that time, Mike had just returned from Duke Seminary and was making a name for himself as a community activist in Berkley. He had been very vocal about racial inequities and violence in the Black community. With a directness I hadn't previously experienced, they told me that my kind of activism had no place in the pulpit or at the microphone in our church.

I was presented with two choices: One, I could have my full-time position reduced down to ten hours a week. This route would include the closure of my Collegiate and Young Professionals ministry office and the placement of my desk in the senior pastor's office (he was the head pastor's son and slated to take over the church) so that I could "relearn what ministry was about." Or two, I could take the offered severance package—a "transitional package," as they called it—to help me transition to my next opportunity.

I chose something else: early retirement. My days as a vocational pastor were over.

I was thirty years old. Up until that point, I had been on a prevocational trajectory toward a role in an institution of religion. I had planned on having my own church someday—my own congregation of thousands. I was the son of a deacon, after all. My father's role was to take care of the institution's needs and care for the congregation, especially those who were sick, elderly, and single moms. This work was in my blood. Working in the church was my birthright.

But my spirit—and my brother, Mike, quite frankly—told me this vision wasn't enough. I had to learn how I could become responsive to a higher calling that needed action. I had started troubling the water, and I couldn't just stop. So I left the safety of the church and went out into the world. I carried a box full of personal belongings from my desk and not much more—other than a lot of questions. I felt compelled to unearth the reasons and the backstory behind why young men in the city of Oakland were killing each other. If I understood the why, then maybe I could help stop the violence.

Discomfort as a Tool

I really didn't know which way to go after I left the church. But within a few months, I got a job with an afterschool program that taught young people of color how to start businesses and become social entrepreneurs. This job offered me an opportunity to be closer to young people who were in trouble, which is what I wanted. So I took it.

The young men in the program had had behavioral issues or episodes of violent behavior at school. They had been placed in my program as a last-ditch effort to try to keep them in school before being tossed out of the district altogether. Our classroom was in an activity room at the Youth Empowerment School, which was a converted junior high. Instead of using the desks, I provided chairs and couches for the kids to hang out and have a relaxed environment.

I used my personal discomfort in this new position as a tool to get closer to theirs. I still carried a deep sense of not belonging to the church anymore—a sense of what it is like to be ostracized. So I used this feeling of being othered as a way to connect with these young people and to try to understand their experiences. I tapped into my sense of being misunderstood and leaned into it. I listened longer than what felt comfortable, allowed them space to be themselves even when I didn't like it, and spent extra time after school to connect with students when they were trying to work through incomplete thoughts about their present and future.

Soon we built a rapport that allowed me to open the door to questions I had been wanting to ask. I was confident that my work of mentoring and pastoring folks in churches allowed me to connect with the hearts of just about anyone. After a couple of encounters, we were vibing on the same level.

One afternoon, as the clock was ticking toward the end of our time together, Spirit called me to connect. I sat with three young teenage brothers before I released them to streets unknown. We started talking about what was going on around them in their neighborhoods. I asked, "Why do you believe the violence is happening?"

One of the young men, tall and astute, about sixteen years old, said, "It's because people are not respecting each other. And if you don't give somebody respect and you don't get respect, then you have to do something to get respect. And if that means you gotta kill somebody, then you gotta kill somebody, as long as you get your respect."

Stunned, I looked at one of the other young men. He was even-keeled, and he couldn't have been more than seventeen. I said, "So you will kill somebody in order to get your respect?"

"Absolutely."

I pointed to the guy sitting next to him and asked, "Would you kill him?"

"Hell, yeah, if he disrespected me. Yeah, I would," he responded without hesitation.

I sat back in my chair. Dressed in my white-collared shirt, jeans, and blazer, I realized all that I had learned during my ten years of pastoring and speaking to hundreds of families within the church was useless. I was underprepared for this moment. Those church folks were dealing with stress like dealing with extramarital affairs, having mothers with alcohol addictions, and not being heard at the dinner table. These were valid difficulties for them, and I like to think I helped them through those. But those types of experiences were worlds away from these young men in front of me and those in their community. My current conversation partners were in such need of baseline respect, honor, and dignity that they were willing to take another human life in order to get it.

I realized I didn't have anything to offer the young men in front of me. I didn't know how to talk to them; I didn't know how to be in relationship with them. All the solutions I thought I had would have fallen flat.

If I was going to do something about the violence in Oakland—if I really wanted to save lives and change lives in the way I felt called to do—I'd have to become a novice, a listener, a learner. I had to step into a world I didn't know, become someone I hadn't been, and start over. I had to strip away everything I thought I knew and become something other than what I was.

Who are you becoming? How willing are you to put in the work necessary to become the new you? Are these questions you can answer with certainty?

In this journey to create a world where the call for radical belonging is answered, each of us needs to be ready, willing, and able to take a long, hard look at ourselves and be fully honest about what we see. We cannot meet the moment dressed as we have always dressed and knowing what we already know. We cannot simply present solutions that feel comfortable for us, soothe our egos, or position us as virtuous. Such solutions are useless to those closest to the pain. We each have to be willing to become something and someone different.

The Gateway to Radical Belonging

Manifesting a world that centers radical belonging begins with our own becoming. Becoming is a journey of formation toward a whole version of self, in community with others. It is a journey of awakening. It recognizes that none of us lives fully awakened to all the challenges happening around us. As individuals who take in new information daily, we are constantly cycling through new and different versions of ourselves.

Radical belonging, however, is not something we can create alone; it is something we must cocreate. It's imperative that when we create a new outcome, it includes the experiences or stories of others. The danger of not cocreating is that we create a world designed for people like us, and that requires the alienation of people different from us. The world is already set up in this way. So cocreation is the catalytic factor that upsets the status quo.

Here's an example: A neighborhood park has fallen into a state of disrepair due to rampant drug use in it. The community has agreed to demolish this park, build apartments on top of it, and create a new park with a new jungle gym across town. A park committee is formed, and the committee has decided that a nice red jungle gym with a ladder, a slide, and a pole for kids to slide down would be a great addition to the new park. Sounds perfect, right? But the committee didn't invite representative voices from the community across town to the table. As a result, they failed to recognize that the neighborhood where they're building this shiny new red jungle gym is near a school for children with disabilities. Many of the neighborhood children would not be able to use the proposed new playground. So not only would it fail to be inclusive, it would also serve as a defense mechanism by the park committee to keep the park "safe" by serving children whom the committee is accustomed to serving. This is not a new outcome in a world where everyone belongs.

Whether we are actually creating belonging must always be determined by those who are most subordinated, or marginalized, within a story. The Powerful don't get to say when we've achieved belonging; that must always be determined by those who are closest to the pain.

In the example of the playground, the children with disabilities and their parents should determine what a playground that signals belonging looks like. In organizational settings, belonging will never be defined by those who have the most power in an organization, such as owners, board members, or C-suite executives; belonging will always be defined by those who have the least. Within a family dynamic, belonging can't be defined by those who have the cultural positions of greatest influence and power in the family; belonging will be defined by those who have the least. Within our society, cocreating is not going to be facilitated by those who are most privileged by past and present institutionalized systems; it will be facilitated by those who are most disadvantaged by the systems. Belonging, for the Powerful and Privileged, requires first hearing from and listening closely to—and then including—those harmed by sustained systems that were built hundreds of years ago and continue to exist today.

To guide you along this journey of becoming—and so that we can ultimately cocreate space for radical belonging—we'll use my 5As framework. The 5As are part developmental theory, part personal and communal formation. The 5As are Awareness, Accountability, Articulation, Advocacy, and Activation. They form a continuum along which we can transform and evolve, and they can lead us toward authentic, radical belonging.

Awareness

Awareness is realizing we have obstruction spots and knowing we must address them. Awareness involves taking in new data, new experiences, and new encounters that we have not had before. We begin to open our eyes to see differently and to hear differently about things that we have not personally experienced.

When I got involved in the work to reduce violence, I didn't understand how people could actually pick up a gun and shoot one of their neighbors in the community. I didn't realize what it felt like to live in those communities and to feel the level of depression, anxiety, and stress of not having access to resources. I had to learn to take in those new experiences, and doing so took time. Committing to awareness meant I had to get into new relationships with new people. I had to position myself in new places. When I engaged in night walks, I would put myself into a new practice. The night walks were designed to close the distance among those engaged in gun violence, those affected by it, and those who weren't. Every Friday evening at 7:00 p.m., I would lead a group of anywhere between twenty-five and one hundred community members though neighborhoods to carry three messages: We love you. The gun violence must stop. Can we learn more about your needs so we can support you? These groups were multiracial, often including members from churches across the city. During several later-night walks, between 11:00 p.m. and 1:00 a.m., about six other ministers and I would walk in the areas where shootings had happened over the last month. We would talk with brothers on the corners, and we'd listen, hard, to what they were telling us. I was trying to take in a new story about those who were close to the violence so that I could have a new story too. I needed a new way of actually seeing the problem that I so desperately wanted to change.

But it also meant I had to do more. I had to discipline myself to read the books, study the articles, and do my own personal work to begin to understand this issue. I had to understand not just the cultural dynamics that led to people being violent; I also had to understand the structural dynamics and the history. I had to learn about redlining and the globalization of the economy and other forces that caused the dynamics that led so many people to see violence as the only way to respond. I learned that communities that did not feel protected by police departments sometimes created a culture of vigilantism and that people who were engaged in violence weren't doing so because they were somehow less human or more prone to violence or because they wanted to fail each other. If they engaged in violence, they usually did so because they had tried to navigate and survive in a system that was failing them again and again.

Growing in awareness means coming with a growth mindset, an open mindset. Awareness means knowing enough about someone else's story that we can actually participate in a solution and subsequently create belonging.

Accountability

With our new awareness, we choose to acknowledge and be held accountable for the ways we have been complicit with the status quo when it comes to power, privilege, and bias. Accountability must happen before we can actively discover opportunities to engage to make the world as it should be.

I took my own steps toward accountability when I recognized that my personal background did not help me confront sexism and the oppression of women in our society. I was raised in a very patriarchal space: a religious space that did not celebrate women in leadership positions or being up front in teaching and speaking roles. So, that created an absolute false reality where I learned that it is okay for men to dominate the space, the conversation, the energy. I am embarrassed to remember one time when I was a young man and visiting a church. When I found that a woman was going to preach, in an act of protest, I stood up and walked out. I believed I should not sit in a place where I was going to be taught by a woman. Now, it might be easy for me to let myself off the hook and say, "Well, I was twenty years old. I didn't know any better." But not knowing better is not an acceptable excuse. I should have done better.

As I became the father of three daughters, I finally began to see the impact of gender injustice on women from the time they enter this world. Women experience the politicization of their bodies and their very presence in the world. I realized I had to take some personal accountability for the way in which my own sexism, and the ways in which I participated in patriarchy, had created a less safe world for them and many other women. I had to recognize that. I had to take some personal responsibility for not only not being part of the solution but actually being part of the problem.

But we can't get stuck there. We can't let ourselves off the hook, thinking that being a part of the problem somehow means we get to just retreat back into silence. Accountability means we take ownership of the fact we have been complicit in other people's harm and marginalization and we need to do something about it. Accountability can be a catalytic agent. We need to come to terms with our own complicity before we begin to address inequity. Accountability is a critical step to take on our journey of becoming.

Articulation

When we live and work and play and worship at a distance from someone who is the perceived other, we often develop a way of talking about them. And usually, the way we talk about it isn't a way that humanizes them. At times, we objectify them or cause them to not be seen in ways they desire to be seen. People who are marginalized often model for us how to tell their stories. The third of the 5As, articulation, means figuring out how to communicate our story, other people's stories, and our collective story. Articulation means being able to talk about how othering and oppression are happening in communities. It's about learning the language of the othered and learning to speak about systemic harm in ways that reflect how communities are speaking about their own harm. It's a call to not colonize or co-opt how marginalized groups speak about their lived experience; it's the invitation to follow their leadership in language.

Back in about 2010, I was sitting at a Starbucks in downtown Oakland on 8th and Washington, and at that time, I was just starting to do some community work. A few days earlier, I happened to run into a brother in West Oakland who said he wanted to follow up and have a one-to-one meeting. So we met at this Starbucks. We were having a good time, talking about the things we hoped could happen in West Oakland for the uplift of everyone. At a certain point, I could tell he was really dialed in and feeling connected, and he said, "I need to stop for a minute."

I said, "Okay, what's the problem?"

He said, "I need you to know something about me. I'm sixty-two years old. I'm gay, and I'm HIV-positive."

I reached across the table, grabbed his hands, and said, "Okay, brother. I got you. Let's go ahead and keep talking." As we talked, I learned more and more about what he had experienced in his life. To navigate his circles, which at that time made no space for people like him, he had had to tell particular people that he did not identify as gay and that he didn't know HIV-positive folks, even though neither of those was his true experience. So now, he told me, he felt compelled to tell people this on the front end. He had experienced the trauma of getting far along in relationships with people, only for them to see who he was and subsequently break off the relationship.

The more I spent time with this brother, the more I realized I needed to learn how to talk about the harmful impact those of us in the straight community often have on our LGBTQ+ relatives and HIV-positive communities. Some of us say we don't *intend* to other LGBTQ+ loved ones—but still, it was becoming clear to me that our own fears and biases lead us to inflict harm. I needed to learn to articulate a story to other people in the straight community about how unsafe LGBTQ+ people often feel. I needed to figure out a way to articulate to my own community the urgency of expanding our circle of human concern.

Articulation allows us to show up differently because of the accountability we've taken. It then empowers us with the ability to talk about other communities that we may not necessarily see ourselves as a part of and communicate the ways they are impacted. At that point, we're able to really begin to make the world a safer place for them. Lifting up the stories of those who have been othered begins to shift hearts and minds.

Advocacy

Advocacy is how we stand up for others in the fight and work toward structural belonging for the Persecuted and

Prevented. This might involve people with no disabilities showing up at a public meeting to ensure there's funding for communities with disabilities or men supporting the concerns of women colleagues in a board meeting. Maybe it's joining a protest about the expansion of human rights or speaking up for a family member who is seen as a problem. Advocacy is how we support the perceived "other" through taking action in service to their needs.

It's one thing for us to care about people who are being impacted and harmed. But advocacy takes it to the next level. I don't have to have your lived experience in order to leverage my voice in support of ensuring that you receive the same opportunities, if not more, than people in my own group do.

I've had to think about the role of advocacy when learning to advocate on behalf of our incarcerated sisters and brothers and relatives. I used to think that if you do the crime, you got to do the time. But slowly I began recognizing that the story of incarceration is much more nuanced than that. I had to learn the ways the system of mass incarceration has been weaponized against Black and brown people and poor communities, how inequality means people don't have a fair chance to access opportunities and to make good choices. I had to begin to see how hard it was for some people to find supportive programs when they suffered from addiction or to have restorative opportunities and second chances, instead of a punitive response, when they made mistakes.

Eventually, I became an advocate. Now when I was in the spaces where formerly incarcerated people were not able to be, I would advocate for them. I'd use my voice to ensure

I was speaking to the Powerful and the Privileged and demanding resources for those incarcerated and formerly incarcerated, the Persecuted and Prevented.

I joined some protests and canvassed in the community to pass a big piece of legislation that would enfranchise a lot of Black and brown people who, because they had been incarcerated, had lost their opportunity for civic engagement. We worked to change the law so that people who had committed low-level crimes—usually while struggling with addiction or poverty—would get opportunities to change their lives rather than get years in prison.

At times, using my voice in this way caused uncomfortable conversations with people who had the power to adjust the dial and create opportunities for formerly incarcerated individuals but who had chosen not to do so. It meant troubling the water on behalf of those who were being sidelined and subordinated. Advocacy is how we leverage the power and privilege that we have in service to those who don't.

Activation

Activation is what happens toward the end of the process, after you have engaged in the arduous work of raising your own awareness, becoming accountable for your own complicity, learning to articulate the dynamics, and becoming an advocate. Now you're inviting others to follow the model that you have leaned into about what it means to show up for the Persecuted and Prevented. Activation is bringing people into awareness and helping them start the journey toward radical belonging. It's moving more people into the space where they can see and hear across difference.

You must go through all of the first four As before getting to activation. Do not go directly from awareness to activation! Failure to go through the other parts of the process will lead to a lot of virtue signaling and tokenism. It can also condition you to show up the "right way" but only for appearances. Put simply, you need to *become* before you can *do*; otherwise, you might end up caring more about how you look than about actually seeing other people for who they are. You need to actually go through that ontological process of becoming: learning what it means to take responsibility and finding ways to up your game, how you communicate, and how you show up for those who have been marginalized.

By the time you get to the end of this formation journey, you've likely got access to relationships and resources, as well as both successes and failures. You've got stories that you can use to help more people get into the work of radical belonging. I only entered the activation phase when, years later, my leadership transitioned from direct contact with our loved ones in the streets to building the capacity of those seeking to get involved. It took me time to get to a place where I could talk in a relatable, authentic way to ministers and other Black people closer to the bourgeois class than to those closest to the pain. I could talk to them about my own sense of vulnerability, which I felt so strongly when I got engaged in the work, and I could invite them to think about what it would mean for them to sacrifice.

The work of activation is bringing people into the story after we made some sacrifices and walked the journey ourselves.

By adhering to the 5As on your personal journey of becoming, you make a conscious choice to unlearn the behaviors, thinking, and ways of being that keep the Prevented and Persecuted held down in the quadrants they are currently in. You choose to instead determine how you, as someone who exists in the Powerful or Privileged quadrants, can work to bridge the treacherous gap that exists.

When we move too fast toward dealing with structures, we don't leave enough time for our hearts and minds to catch up. I once talked to a police executive about the debate over passing policies and legislation to change policing versus changing hearts and minds along the way. "Culture eats structure for breakfast," he told me. And I see his point. Yes, structures and policies and laws need to be changed, and future chapters will help us look at some of that macro-level work. But examples abound of individuals and corporations rushing to advocacy and activation without doing the long, slow work of changing themselves and their culture. After George Floyd's murder in 2020, for example, many corporations jumped to advocacy and activation without going through the journey. "Black Lives Matter" became a decal found on most brands, and people donated millions of dollars. But now those hashtags are gone, the donations have ceased, and many Black people within those very corporations are sharing with me that nothing actually changed in the culture of their companies.

On our journey of becoming, we learn, slowly, to dismantle the status quo by listening, learning, and committing to radical belonging for us all. The risk of not doing this courageous work is that we change everything and nothing at the same time.

3

Build a Bridge

I stood on the corner of Canfield Drive and West Florissant Street in Ferguson, Missouri, in the summer of 2014. Cheyenne, a small-framed, dark-skinned young woman with gold streaks in her hair, was talking to our group of protesters with all the unwavering confidence, fearlessness, and determination of a seasoned civil rights leader. She must have been about fifteen years old.

Like her teenage comrades who filled the makeshift tents that created a colorful backdrop behind her, Cheyenne was committed to staying in the streets and protesting the killing of eighteen-year-old Michael Brown for as long as it took to get justice. At this time, that meant the arrest of police officer Darren Wilson, who had shot and killed the unarmed Black teenager on August 9. Many of the parents and guardians of the young people in the group had warned them "If you go out, you can't come back" in an effort to force them to stay home. They went anyway.

These young people, who called themselves the Lost Voices, weren't part of any formal organization. They weren't operating from any playbook. They had simply decided that this moment was too important for them to stay home and do nothing. They were pulled by the sense of fed-upness that only the Prevented and the Persecuted know when the weight of trauma, disregard, and injustice becomes too much to bear. That insistence within your spirit that enough is enough, that you must do something, even if it means sacrificing yourself. I was struck not only by Cheyenne's assuredness that what she and the others were doing was right but also by her faith that *because* it was right, support would show up. "We just believe that because we're doing the right thing, people will help us," she told me. And that happened: support showed up for them in the form of strangers who believed in their mission.

That day, I was one of those strangers. I took Cheyenne and some of the others to get Chinese food, as she requested, and on the ride there, she talked about how so many of the folks in her community were dealing with a debtor's prison, petty fines, and all sorts of other insidious tactics that St. Louis County officials used to oppress the Black and poor people there. So for Cheyenne and the others, the protests weren't just about Mike Brown. The uprising was them saying, "I'm tired of seeing my parents lose their jobs. I'm tired of bad schools. I'm tired of being exploited and oppressed. So we're going to show up."

When I first arrived in Ferguson, the protests had already been going on for two weeks. I didn't know what to think, what to expect, or what to do exactly. This was my first time being a part of activism that took the fight to the streets. Before that, my battleground had been predominantly classrooms, activity rooms, and churches, working with young people who were in danger of becoming a part of violence in the community.

Along with a change of clothing, I brought my own biases about what proper activism should look like. I thought it should be planned, thoughtful, polished, collaborative, with all opposing parties seated at the table. So young people sleeping in tents on the street, depending on the kindness of strangers to sustain them with food and water while they were out there protesting every evening, it was all foreign to me. Witnessing a young man with face tattoos cursing at a crowd of protesters to gather before they marched—and then insisting that they all pause for a moment of prayer beforehand—unnerved me. Even while I protested alongside a group on West Florissant Street, which connected Ferguson and St. Louis, I felt kind of like I was having an out-of-body experience because everything was unfamiliar to me. What I was doing was unfamiliar to me. These people were unfamiliar to me. Even the St. Louis accent was unfamiliar.

But I chose to sit with the discomfort brought on by the unfamiliarity. That unease was becoming a part of my evolution, and I was learning that discomfort is a signal to listen to rather than disregard. The paradigm within me was shifting: from seeing young people as those who needed to be helped to seeing them as people who could lead. It was very humbling for me to stand there and gain knowledge from a fifteen-year-old girl. I was old enough to be Cheyenne's dad, but she knew more about what was happening to poor Black people than I did. I had to confront my own imperialism and paternalism, and I had to give up this notion of "I'm the Black preacher; I know best. Let me lead." There's actually more blessing in the following of others than there is in the leading. As much as I had tried to get that mindset out of me over the several years since I had stopped pastoring, it was still there. I know it is still there today, and I hope I will continue to become.

My time in Ferguson forced me to look at my work as an advocate for radical belonging in a new way. It made me reassess my approach. To do so, I had to let go of everything I thought I knew and be willing to become a novice. I did more listening and less talking. And as a result of following these unlikely leaders, I got a lot of my humanity back. I was so inspired by the courage they had, particularly because it was courage I didn't feel like I had access to. In them, I witnessed the courage to risk it all in the service of creating a better world for all of us. I became someone different—someone with a much deeper understanding of the Persecuted and Prevented in those communities. I got insight into not only what was happening to them but what was hurting them.

This is the power of following the lead of people you may have previously othered, whether consciously or not. Those young people baptized me into activism. They were, in essence, my imams, rabbis, reverends, and pastors in this work. They showed me in real terms—as activist Glenn E. Martin reminds us—that people closest to the pain are the people closest to the solution. If only we, the Powerful and the Privileged, would just shut up and listen.

Put Yourself at Risk

Systems created by the Powerful and enjoyed by the Privileged have othered people who are Prevented and Persecuted. They have done this by delegitimizing their voices, their expressions, and their testimonies. In Ferguson, I had to *re*legitimize the people who had been delegitimized to me.

Even though I may have been proximate to young brothers during the gun-violence work I did in Oakland, I still did not see them as leaders. I saw them as these young brothers who were shooting each other. And we—the leaders in the community—must help them, right? But in Ferguson, I began to ask: Who better than these brothers to lead *us*? They understand what's happening on a deeper level than any of us can imagine. We should be there to support them and be in the struggle *with* them.

If you are really going to struggle against white supremacy, structural racism, racialized othering, or any other form of othering, you have to know something: there is a real cost to this work. This cost goes beyond simply learning how to say the right things or retweet, repost, or reshare those things when they are trending. It is not about putting signs in your windows or releasing a corporate statement on your company's website saying "Black Lives Matter" or "Stop Asian Hate."

Solidarity, as Ferguson taught me, requires sacrifice. It means putting your power and privilege on the line based upon what the Persecuted and the Prevented are asking you to do. It is saying to the othered, "I see that you are negatively impacted by this, and I am going to put myself at risk because you are already at risk. I am going to be with you and your struggle. I'm not going to care for you from afar."

My time in Ferguson reinforced for me the notion that in order for us all to be welcomed into the circle of human concern, we have to close the gaps between us. We have to build bridges that create channels for "us" and "them" to become "we." When we are the Powerful and Privileged, we may tolerate the existence of these gaps because they keep us comfortable. Maybe those gaps allow us to keep our jobs, or to keep being invited to the cookout, or to practice virtue signaling and promote our wokeness without getting our hands dirty. But just as solidarity takes sacrifice, bridging the gaps takes courage.

Bridging is the practice of finding our interrelatedness with the other. For some of us, this will be personally challenging. To find interrelatedness—getting people to listen, getting people to stop hurting others, getting people to act with some modicum of humanity—may be the entry point to where you are in your journey because it is where you are feeling the most pain. But even with all its discomfort, bridging is exactly where you are supposed to be. It is a continual state of being.

The beauty of bridging is it helps us to tap back into the most powerful source we have: love. The great cultural critic and activist bell hooks writes, "All the great movements for social justice in our society have emphasized a love ethic." Reigniting the often-smothered ability to develop love and deep empathy for the other gives us power to cross the streets of separation, division, and difference and ultimately allows us to create radical belonging. Cynics like to diminish the power of love; they say it doesn't have any real ability to change conditions. I say we're here to prove them wrong.

Dr. john powell says that bridging is the practice we must enact once we've put ourselves at the table and are ready to co-create with one another. Bridging means participating in dialogue and structured engagement that enable us to see our differences as something positive rather than negative and to build new systems and structures that are anchored in belonging. Our job is to keep expanding our circle of human concern so that it may hold our own perspective and that of another. This means that structural work must be accompanied by *cultural* work: confronting implicit biases and prioritizing a movement of deep relational work to create a country where literally everybody can belong.

Sometimes when we are building bridges, however, things don't work out. Sometimes, just like in life, things break.

Breaking

When we begin to "other" people—as Dr. powell explains, when a group turns inward and against the "outsider," pushing away from other groups who are seen as dangerous or as less than—breaking occurs. Breaking happens when we stop traveling down the path of understanding: when communication stops, when listening stops, when seeing others for who and what they are stops. "The otherness and threat of the out-group can be used to build psychological or physical walls. It tells the other, 'You are not one of us. You don't belong and you should not get the same public resources or attention and regard that my group gets,'" Dr. powell writes.

Instead of breaking, Dr. powell suggests, we need to take the step of bridging. What bridging does is neither *denied* because of difference nor *disappeared* because of difference. Bridging creates space to recognize difference and then begin to identify how we use that difference as fuel to cocreate a new society, a new world, a new organization, a new culture that is wide enough and large enough to hold our difference.

Hear me on this: Bridging is not about avoiding difference. Bridging is about naming difference and then doing the hard work of identifying how that difference creates opportunities for a new outcome. When it comes to race, for example, bridging calls on us not to be color*blind*—the claim frequently made by white people that "I don't see color." Bridging calls us, rather, to be *color brave*. Mellody Hobson, president and co-CEO of Ariel Investments and chairwoman of Starbucks Corporation, coined this term. She writes, "We cannot afford to be color blind. We have to be color brave. We have to be willing, as teachers and parents and entrepreneurs and scientists, we have to be willing to have proactive conversations about race with honesty and understanding and courage, not because it's the right thing to do, but because it's the smart thing to do, because our businesses and our products and our science, our research, all of that will be better with greater diversity." I am a Black man. I can't deny that, and I won't. Just as you identify with whoever you are. This work—of naming difference and working to identify how that difference creates opportunities—does take bravery, and it is crucial in this time.

Here's the thing, though: Bridging work is strenuous. As I once heard author and social activist bell hooks warn,

"The most challenging thing about bridges is that they're made to be walked on." In other words, the bridge doesn't get celebrated; the bridge exists to connect point A to point B. When you are doing bridging work, people aren't always going to see what you're doing as helpful. They will misunderstand you. They will judge you. They will say it will never work or that you're a sellout. This is true no matter whether you're doing bridging work with the young people in the community, or bridging with the police, or bridging with the movement, or bridging with evangelicals, or bridging with LGBTQ+ relatives. People are going to walk on you.

Yet in the same way that architects built monumental cathedrals hundreds of years ago that they knew they would never get to see completed, you have to view the work you are doing today—the bridging—as serving what I call the "cathedral plan." You're putting in work for generations to come, even though you may never personally witness or experience the beautiful results of your work. This is true of many activists and community organizers—people we might call *emancipation practitioners*—who were part of the civil rights movement. Even though they envisioned a world that included the rights and possibilities many of us experience today, many of them did not live to experience those rights and possibilities themselves. They knew this would be the case—and they still remained committed to the work of belonging. They bridged anyway.

How to Build a Bridge

So how do we begin to bridge across difference? The first step is to gain an awareness of the power you, personally, hold in any given situation. Pioneering legal scholar Dr. Kimberlé Crenshaw says people are often disadvantaged—or advantaged—by multiple sources of oppression: race, class, gender identity, religion, and other identity markers. It's important to know that most people do not fall into just one category of identity, which means that none of us is just one thing. Many of us don't exist in just one quadrant all the time. Many people are subordinated in some contexts and advantaged in others. A white woman might be paid less than her male colleague because of gender injustice while also receiving preferential treatment by a police officer because of her whiteness. Dr. Crenshaw called this notion—that our identities can overlap to intensify or blunt discrimination—intersectionality.

Context is everything with bridging, just as context is everything with power. To keep it real with you, some of my bridging experiences functioned because I was *not* the most disadvantaged person in the group. In my work with community groups, I was often positioned with a bit of power—whether that came from my physical stature, gender identity, operational function, community standing, or profession. Depending on the context, those elements of power gave me more margin to work as I was seen as having the credibility necessary to bridge.

While all must be willing to come to a table and seek to understand the other, I believe the greater responsibility for bridging lies with the more powerful person in any given dynamic. The Persecuted and the Prevented might, out of habit, tend to take on the responsibility of "understanding" the other because they've had to. Black folks are expected to laugh at racist jokes and are chided with "We're just having fun" when they don't laugh. Or when a woman is talked over by men in meetings and then speaks up about it, she is told, "Don't be so sensitive." Therefore, the onus of responsibility for bridging lies with the Powerful. I've often been told that this is a false notion; people tell me I should say instead that bridging work is the responsibility of everyone, equally, all the time. Still, I believe placing the responsibility for bridging on the Persecuted and Prevented—especially in certain contexts—can be an act of violence, even if unintended.

Those with more power and privilege should carry the burden of the bridging, and restorative justice often must play a role in bridging, particularly when there has been harm. Expecting groups who have experienced harm to bridge without healing contributes to more violence and should be resisted by marginalized communities at all costs.

The second step to bridging is to seek to understand the other beyond what you think you know. Within this step, your main function is to recognize the difference of the other, sit in the tension caused by anxiety of the unknown, stay at the table, and choose not to break. This is about being willing to see the world from someone else's point of view—without approving it and without affirming it. But we listen from the perspective of simply acknowledging it as a point of view that another human being holds.

When I first met Bill in 2012, he was a forty-eight-year-old white evangelical pastor, former police officer, and hard-right conservative. He had begun a process of deconstruction a couple of years before he met me, after engaging in some bridging work with Muslim leaders in Pakistan in 2007 and Black matriarchs in Haiti in 2008. He had shown up there after the earthquakes with his relief organization to provide aid. Those relationships and experiences began to challenge him in the way he saw the world and the ideological constructs he had adopted. While it was easier for Bill to see injustice abroad, he struggled, as a white man benefiting from the reality of American imperialism and racism, to see it at home. But he was committed to becoming and bridging.

We began a friendship, and he and I both had to work on listening to each other's points of view, which were at odds. Soon, Bill began accepting my invitation to show up in places where Black people were—but to do so to learn rather than lead. He traveled with me to the fiftieth anniversary of the March on Washington on the National Mall in 2013, and he came with me to Ferguson the next year. One night during the Ferguson uprising, Bill made a choice to bridge, even though he still wasn't sure he belonged in the movement.

Bill and I were heading back to our hotel when a conflict erupted between the Ferguson protesters and the Ferguson Police Department. We had just dined with one of the young men who was protesting Michael Brown's killing, and we were dropping him off before we headed back to the hotel for the night. As we were driving, my brother, Mike, called and asked if I was still in Ferguson; I told him yes. He told me to get over to West Florissant to help the young people there. He was watching a livestream on Twitter and was concerned something really bad was about to happen.

So I hit a U-turn in the middle of the street and sped down to West Florissant. The protest was happening right in front of the Ferguson Market, where Mike Brown had been killed. As we pulled up, we saw about one hundred young people standing face to face with about twenty police officers. I pulled into a parking lot across the street from where they were gathered, put the car in park, and jumped out. One practice we clergy-activists adopted in Ferguson was putting our bodies between the police and the young people. We figured that we could play an important role in preventing more violence and keeping everyone safe by putting ourselves in the middle. So I ran across the street without thinking much about what Bill would do.

That night, as Bill watched me run across the street, he had a choice. He could have stayed in the car, where he'd be safe. But sure enough, he came walking behind me. He joined me in the middle of the fray as we talked to protesters and police officers and helped to deescalate the situation.

Later, Bill would tell me he wasn't sure he should get out of the car and cross the street. Given who he was and who he had been, he wasn't sure he belonged in the crowd that night. But he was willing to take a risk, cross the street, and do what he could.

Now, some ten years into this journey together, Bill and I are like brothers. Together we are taking risks and learning how to bridge.

When Breaking Leads to Bridging

Sometimes, though, breaking happens before bridging can. I had to learn this lesson—that breaking can lead to bridging—when I met Jabari, a brother who has provided me with one of the most transformative relationships I've ever had. We are comrades in the work we do for the community in Oakland. Jabari is now a violence-prevention consultant who works across the country to support peacemaking efforts. But we had to break several times in order for this powerful bridge to be built between us. We have sustained many fractures along the way.

Jabari, who is forty-two years old, grew up in East Oakland. After losing his mother at a young age, he ended up in foster homes and seeking validation on the streets. Jabari shared his origin story on my podcast, *An Invitation to Become*. "I believed there were predators and there were prey out there on the streets," he told me. "Either you were going to be a predator, or you were going to be prey, and I've seen the prey not take it so easily. So I figured being a predator would be better than being the prey."

I met Jabari back in 2013 at a call-in in Oakland. Call-ins were part of our violence-reduction work in the community. At Ceasefire, we would identify those who were at the highest risk to either shoot somebody or be shot. Then we'd facilitate a conversation by bringing in them and their loved ones, who, we knew from the research and from experience, were likely to experience violence. Together, as a group, we'd try to do some bridging and compel these young brothers to make different choices. We didn't want them to keep dying.

To get these young men to the call-in, we collaborated with the Oakland police. But our strategy for getting them into a room together was embarrassingly flawed. I knew it, and Jabari knew it. The police would roll up on them at their homes and their moms' homes. There'd be eight, nine, and ten squad cars deep. With guns drawn, the police officers would "invite" them to a meeting to "change their lives."

As you might guess, this tactic did not go over well.

Jabari was ordered by his probation officer to attend the call-in or face jail time. When he arrived that first day, he was wearing a leather coat, baggy jeans, a dark-brown sweater, and black-and-white Jordans. I remember that even though it wasn't cold that day, he had on multiple layers of clothing, which I later learned is a tactic for concealing weapons while on the street. Jabari kept looking over his shoulder at the door, nervous that the whole thing was a setup and that he was going to jail, but he attempted to conceal his anxiety by playing it off with jokes, a smile revealing gold grills in his mouth.

I was sitting at a table, wearing a light-blue Cityteam corporate shirt tucked into my navy slacks with my dark-brown Cole Hahn shoes. I watched Jabari just as I watched all the young brothers who were filing into the room. I was trying to get a read on who might need extra help in being at ease or who might need support to make the decision toward peace over more violence. When he noticed me, Jabari pointed at me and said, "You gon' help me!"

He didn't know me. But in that moment, Jabari directly called on me—in this case, the Powerful and the Privileged—to step up. From that point on, I attempted to bridge with Jabari, even when it was uncomfortable for both of us, even when he wasn't feeling it, even when, quite frankly, it just wasn't working. There was an obstacle between us, one that we both had to commit to bridging across.

"I had to shake my addiction to certain behavior," Jabari told me in our podcast interview, reflecting on his own journey of formation. "I had to let go of what I was used to doing in order to accept something new. I was conditioned to living a certain type of way. I was conditioned to think, 'Only white people go eat at the restaurant and eat strawberry salads and cross their legs and put the napkin on their lap.' I'm outside thugging. We're eating spreads on the block, and you'd be lucky you can make it to McDonald's if you ain't trying to sell off your bundle fast enough. So just looking at the way you were living and being afraid that I deserved it, I think, was my biggest challenge."

Jabari also shared that he had to learn how to manage his expectations for how I might be able to help him. Together we learned that the inverse of othering someone else is "saming" them: erasing the possibility of difference. Saming is believing all humans are alike despite cultural differences; it often comes out as truisms like "I don't see race" or "Why can't we all just get along?" Both othering and saming are destructive.

Even we, as Black men, sometimes same each other, thinking all our experiences align. When we realize they don't, breaking can often occur. As Jabari reflected on the podcast:

> I think it's just the fact that we can oftentimes look at somebody and assume, "Okay, this a Black man, and all Black men go through the same thing." You feel me? We all experience the same drama. And that wasn't the situation. I was expecting you to understand everything that I was going through, and by me seeing your position, your status, seeing an educated brother, [I thought] you would be able to find the solution to my problem: by researching, education, finding a friend, or some type of way. Like, you could find the answer to my problem

because you have the answer to all these other problems that's going on in our community. And I think that was my biggest pull on you.

Then when I was bringing certain things to you, like, for instance, "Bruh, help me with this child support stuff." And you're like, "Bruh, I'ma try my best." But when I sit back now and really look at it, you ain't never had to go through child support. So I was asking you to help me with a situation or a problem that you never experienced, and I think that that was like vinegar and water. I was pouring in a problem that you weren't able to hold for me at that point in time.

For my part, I didn't completely understand the journey Jabari was on. When I met him, he was trying hard to reintegrate into society and become a "regular person" after years of living by the code of the streets. Even though I had spoken to hundreds of young men who were part of our community groups over the years, I had not yet been close, one on one, to anyone with Jabari's life experiences. I thought exposing him to new things was the fastest way to reach him and form a bond.

Through my relationship with him, and because of the bridge that now exists between us, I learned that for people to authentically belong, it's not just helping a person find a job, and it's not just lingo. It's not helping people assimilate into your own culture, and it's not "Let's go on a trip so I can expose you to some place you've never been." It's much more than that. Bridging is less like winning someone over to your way. It's more like dying and being born again.

Jabari and I both did the difficult and uncomfortable work of building a bridge and establishing a relationship with each other that evolved over time. I realize now that if you're going to bridge across difference, the most fundamental thing a person has to have is patience. You and the person with whom you are bridging can't judge the success of the bridging based on your timetable. You can't rush progress because we're all starting in different places. But you also can't give up.

Our society is set up for you to stay with the people who are like you, to have your existing perspective reaffirmed, and to distrust anyone who is different from you. So bridging doesn't seem necessary. Additionally, bridging raises a lot of suspicion from folks who are within your quadrant concerning why you're bridging ("Why would you go talk to them?"). When people don't understand what bridging really is, they may think you are compromising, or selling out, or giving in, or even becoming a traitor to the truth as they see it.

That's what makes this step difficult. We're conditioned to be afraid of difference. This fear, whether it comes from societal standards or your tribal identity, causes obstacles to bridging. We're all operating with a trust deficit, and we have to work through mistrust to understand one another. But mistrust causes dehumanization. It causes us to think that someone like Jabari might deserve to be locked up instead of lifted up. It makes us think that the person with a lesser degree at our workplace has less to offer or a perspective not worth listening to.

If you are among the Powerful or the Privileged, you might be thinking, "What will I lose if I actually engage and begin to bridge with those who are Persecuted and Prevented?" This is the wrong question. As the Powerful and the Privileged, you should ask yourself, "What will I stand to gain?"

Some additional questions I want you to consider are: What are the kinds of structures, stories, and future realities we could build that we might not live long enough to see realized but that future generations will step into? What kind of imagination is this moment calling on us to have? What kind of table is it calling on us to build? What kind of bridge is it demanding we forge? What kind of relationship will give birth to some new human possibilities—perhaps not for us but for generations down the road?

Systems that oppress humankind stand at the center of my work, and so I am working on ways to have less work. Bridging is one of those ways.

4

Confront Your Biases

Even advocates for belonging can let our biases get the best of us. It has happened to me. This didn't happen in most cases because I didn't know better; it happened because the pull of my bias, in those moments, was fueled by fear, self-preservation, or the sheer habit of othering those who appear different from me. I will not claim I have no bias, and I will not allow you to do so either. Having the courage to confront our own biases is one of the key steps to creating a world of radical belonging—a world where everyone is welcomed, just as they are, into the circle of human concern.

Dr. Jennifer Eberhardt, author of the book *Biased: Uncovering the Hidden Prejudice That Shapes What We See, Think, and Do*, is a psychology professor at Stanford University who studies the subtle, complex, largely unconscious, and yet deeply ingrained ways that individuals racially code and categorize people. Her work focuses on associations between race and crime. Biases, Dr. Eberhardt explains, are "the beliefs and the feelings we have about social groups that can influence our decision making and our actions, even when we're not aware of it."

When it comes to forming an opinion about something, be it a tall, dark-skinned man walking toward you on the street, or a person pulling something from their pocket "suspiciously," or an individual wearing clothing that represents a particular faith, our cultural knowledge, our social influences, and our prior experiences cause us to make a quick assessment of what we see. This happens before we consciously recognize this assessment is even happening. Our brain is hardwired to categorize our perceptions. Implicit bias refers to the attitudes or stereotypes that affect our understanding, actions, and decisions in an unconscious manner. "The brain needs to sort everything—the food we eat, the furniture we use, whatever," Dr. Eberhardt told *Time* magazine. "We also sort people. That sorting can lead to bias; once we have categories, we have beliefs and feelings about what's in those categories."

Implicit bias happens for us at a very core level—almost instinctively because of how we're triggered around safety and security. In some ways, bias is unavoidable. It is going to show up in your work. It is going to show up in your personal life. Bias is not a trait but a state. So some situations and conditions make you more vulnerable to bias than others. When you feel threatened or fearful, for example, you are more likely to act on your biases than in situations where you are feeling affirmed. The more you understand this, the more you can restrain the power of that bias. Then the issue is trying to figure out what the situations are where bias is more likely to come up. After that, you can determine how to avoid those situations, or how to brace yourself for those situations, or how to slow down in those situations and check yourself.

As hard as you might work to see everyone equally, and despite your genuine well-intended motives to be an ally to those who are othered, some bias will be present in your life. This will likely be true for you more times than not. This should not be a deterrent against the social justice work you do or rattle your commitment to creating a world where everyone belongs. Rather, *knowing* you have unconscious prejudice awakens your awareness, and that awareness will help you create even greater change.

Before you realize this, however, implicit bias can nearly wreck your work. Before I came to learn and understand this, my implicit bias nearly cost me everything.

Don't Believe Your Bias

By 2013, I had taken on a direct leadership role in the Oakland Ceasefire Steering Committee, and we continued to learn about Ceasefire strategies and ways to best assist people most impacted by violence.

We'd made some wonderful progress in reducing gun violence and had developed deep relationships with those we were serving: individuals at the highest risk to commit acts of violence because they were also those at the highest risk of becoming victims of it. Our goal was to get to our people first before law enforcement got to them. Straight up.

This work was extremely stressful, and the stakes were incredibly high. People were dying all the time, and if we weren't hearing about a new death, we were hearing about the funeral or about a person being hunted and locked up for murder. We were in a constant state of collective mourning, and we lived with the pain of trauma that seemed to climb into your body, take up space, and never leave. We were all unpaid volunteers who chose to do this work. Many of us worked full-time jobs during the day and then attended emotionally draining evening meetings that lasted hours, only to drag ourselves home to cold dinners, sleeping children, or dark and lonely apartments. It could be very depressing at times. But the work had to be done. That much we all knew.

One powerful exercise within the Ceasefire strategy was the call-in, which I mentioned in the last chapter. The exercise was based on building shared humanity, holding space, and sitting at the table with one another. The individuals coming to the table were not coming in peace. We brought in young men who had been actively shooting at each other over the past several months. We also invited mothers who had lost their children to the very gun violence in which these young men had been participants. We brought in loved ones who had been former perpetrators of that gun violence. We brought in faith leaders who presided over the funerals and buried the victims of the violence. We also brought in law enforcement partners who had participated in arresting the young men. We brought in the district attorney, and the US attorney, and lawyers who had prosecuted and ensured that these brothers were incarcerated. All had a seat at the table.

One call-in was held at the Lakeshore Avenue Baptist Church. It was a majority-white church just north of the 580 freeway, which essentially separated Oakland between north and south and segregated the haves and have-nots, breaking across race and class. The location was a neutral zone, meaning it was not on anyone's turf, so it was safe for our purposes.

Each call-in would begin with one of us opening the meeting with a caring message. Dr. George Cummings, steering committee cochair and a prominent Oakland faith leader, Assistant Police Chief Paul Figueroa, or I would express to the young men, "We care about you. We want to see you safe. We want you to stop the shooting."

These brothers sat around the table with their heads low, looking down at the floor, barely making eye contact. Some did so in defiance or anger. They felt threatened by law enforcement and were afraid they would go to jail if they didn't attend the call-ins. They didn't want to be there, and their body language communicated that clearly. Others didn't want to be there for other reasons that were not yet evident—but they kept those reasons to themselves. They didn't listen to us, but they tolerated us, serving their time within our presence until it was time to go.

Until, at this particular call-in, Ms. Louise spoke. "I lost my son," she told them, explaining how her son was killed by a stray bullet years before. She looked at them and said to them in absolute terms, "You are all beautiful to me." As she shared her story, she spoke to the young men assembled as if they were her sons too. She spoke with love in her voice tinged by the pain that still racked her body. In a torrent of tears, she told them, "The last thing I want is for something to happen to you and for your mother to go through what I'm going through."

Us, they tolerated. To her, they listened.

Monica spoke that day as well. She was a nurse in the trauma ward at Highland Hospital, Oakland's top trauma center. With a matter-of-factness devoid of the thrill and pacing of medical dramas we see on Netflix, she explained in vivid terms what she saw. She made a clicking, gasping sound to demonstrate a paralyzed gunshot victim choking on their own vomit. "After the first week, all your friends stop showing up, then your girlfriend," she told them. "And after a while you're sitting in that room alone with your mother or maybe your grandmother—if you're lucky." They heard her. They listened. Her message was clear: there is no romance in being shot.

Then Kevin Grant, someone who had been what he called a "career criminal," stood. Kevin, Oakland Unite's violence-prevention coordinator, was a muscular guy in his mid-fifties. Kevin was well known as a peace-broker. He told them he knew what they were going through because he'd been where they were. He'd been incarcerated, and he'd lived a life of crime. "We don't want to bury you all," he said. "We want to make you feel safe. I am sorry you had to feel that you needed to pick up a gun." To him, they listened.

These young men, whom society had written off as hopeless, listened. They lifted their heads, looked us in the eye, longed for more. They wanted something else for their lives. A group of people cared and showed them, maybe for the first time in their lives, that they belonged. They heard, saw, and felt that these people—who were affected by the violence they had perhaps played a role in inflicting on the community—didn't want them locked up or wiped out. They wanted the best for them.

We found that every time we held one of these call-in meetings—whenever there was a table where our young men were seen as full human beings and provided the kind of support to change their lives—close to 70 percent of them would opt out of the violence immediately. And 80 percent of all who attended signed up for mentor and case-worker services. It felt to us like it was working. The numbers provided empirical evidence to back up our theory that it was working.

After the group call-ins, I had one-on-one follow-up sessions with many of the young men who were present in order to build even deeper relationships: to bridge with them. Each session would teach me something new, both about them and about myself. I recognized we had so much more in common than I had thought—*and* that the differences that did exist required recognition.

For example, many of us loved our mothers, but for some of us, that love was expressed as anger for a multitude of reasons. Maybe we had a fractured relationship with our mother or didn't experience affection from her because she was dealing with her own struggles and life had hardened her so much. Many of us loved a hamburger, but how we were treated once in the restaurant or how much money we had left in our pocket after buying the burger made all the difference in our love for that hamburger. Many of us demanded respect in the workplace, but how we got that respect, as well as what the workplace was, differed.

Now here is where we turn to the story of my implicit bias. As I began bridging with these young men, and as their trust in me grew, some of them began to reveal to me big, disturbing secrets. But these secrets were not about them. They told me that law enforcement officials, including some of the very folks we were sharing the table with at the call-in, were crooked.

The stories they told me were horrifying in scope and nature. They told me that some of the police officers were having orgies with the women in their community and that these men were abusing their power and using their city-appointed authority to take advantage of people. They told me that by holding a table with law enforcement, I was giving cover to them. I was enabling the lack of integrity that had infiltrated their community. Yes, these young men saw that my intention was to stop the violence in the community. Yet they were telling me that a different type of violence was taking place—violence by those who were supposed to *protect* the community.

I listened. But I didn't believe them. I didn't believe them because of my own bias.

After one call-in following these revelations, that same bias prompted me to march over to one of the officers on the command staff. We were of the same religious persuasion, and, in confidence, I shared with him what the young men told me. I just wanted proof it wasn't true. I needed him—another leader, like me—to validate my bias.

"Ben, you know that's not the case," he assured me. "They're just making up stories because they don't want to be held responsible for some of the bad behavior that they're doing."

I listened. And I believed him.

But why? I'd approached him as a means to speak up for the young men, those who had been prevented and persecuted by the status quo. (Wasn't I aligned with them? I was there to help them, after all.) Yet my natural proclivity was to lean toward what was familiar to me, what I knew. By that time, I had seen and heard a lot. I could imagine the scenarios the young men described to me; I knew of women being disadvantaged by men, I knew of coverups and crooked deals, and I knew of all the cruelty that goes with them. What I *didn't* yet know or trust was the perspective of my sources; it was too far away from me.

The police officer and I held a closer perspective, one that comes from the security provided by power and privilege. As a police officer, he had more power and privilege than I did in our context. But we were two men who held status in the community and sat at the heads of tables rather than on the sides. I was influenced by what we had in common—or at least what I *thought* we had in common. Plus, he professed to be a man of God—even of my God. The commonality I felt with him, on a very personal level, became a lens that enabled me to believe what he told me with greater ease. I chose to believe him rather than to believe the young men and what they divulged. I had less anxiety when I believed him; I felt safe.

I did feel some level of safety with the young men too. But it was a sense of comfort that came with the perspective that I was the one in control, the leader in the relationships with them, the protector. My bias caused me to see them through a paternalistic lens: worthy of my help and yet unworthy of my trust. I was willing to lead them but not to follow them. Even though I was saying publicly that they were leaders who could lead the city into peace, I didn't actually believe it at a core level. I still saw myself as the leader.

I can see this now, but I couldn't see it then.

I also had a profound feeling of responsibility toward the young men, and in some cases, we were developing what I would even call friendships. But even though I cared deeply for them, I was still influenced by the differences between us. I was beginning to recognize these young men and see their humanity, yet my bias was still active to the point of not allowing me to listen to them fully. I was suspicious. They had not yet, in my eyes, ascended to a place of being actual cocreative partners with me, with full agency. Based on my preconceived perceptions of them, I still viewed myself as their savior.

On My Block

See, I did not grow up in "the hood." The pain of the communities and people I have intentionally drawn close to as an adult was, during my childhood, far away. I grew up in a middle-class neighborhood in San Francisco, the son of a city bus driver and a schoolteacher. We lived in a house my father bought for twenty-four thousand dollars in 1972 with the GI Bill.

In 2008, I decided to relocate my family to an East Oakland neighborhood that city officials and the press designated "the Kill Zone" because it accounted for 70 percent of the annual murders. The area had been abandoned by economic investment and even police. It was known that if there was a homicide, the Oakland Police Department might not enter the Kill Zone until backup arrived—if at all.

The Kill Zone—which includes Seminary Avenue up to the San Leandro border and is fenced in by the 580 freeway—was a dense area of small homes, multiplexes, and housing projects with a few thoroughfares full of liquor stores and fast-food chains. To me, it seemed like a war zone—barbed wires interwoven atop once-nice chain-linked fences; boarded-up shops with vintage signage from years ago that lay discarded next to those still hanging on; and graffiti, which had been artful once upon a time, covering most surfaces. All this resided in this area, alongside the exhausted and frightened community of people who were trying to survive despite the violence that enveloped them.

To me, East Oakland was the epicenter of the pain, and it was where I, someone who was all about advocating for peace, needed to go. I needed to see it with my own eyes. Even though I was Black, I would only later realize my own bias against neighborhoods like this and the people who live in them. It emerged for me even as I stepped out of my gray '94 Mercedes Benz onto my new street. I was there not as a voyeur to observe how "the other half" lived but as a student, to witness it with curiosity and a desire to learn. I was there to be immersed within a new community so that I could figure out what to do, how I could be most helpful.

Was I scared? Hell yes! This wasn't just about me. At that time, my daughters were eight, five, and four; I was a father and a husband with a family to protect. I had to know I was making the right decision. My wife, Gynelle, and I prayed about it before making the move, and we were convinced we were doing the right thing. We walked forward with faith. Still, I had my concerns.

We had chosen a two-story, red-brick 1920s house on 60th Avenue as our new home. On one of the last days before we closed on the house, my family and I went for a final visit. As we pulled up to what was to be our new home, I looked out my car window and saw one of our new neighbors I would later come to know as Blaine. Blaine, wearing what appeared to be swimming trunks, was casually sitting on a lawn chair in the middle of the street, blocking all the traffic. He was literally sunbathing in the middle of the street, in East Oakland, in the middle of the day.

After taking in Blaine and trying to make sense of everything I was witnessing, I looked at my wife and thought, *We're moving into the hood.* My bias, which was always embedded somewhere within me—as it is within all of us—began to rear its ugly head.

On our first fully moved-in night in our new home, Gynelle decided to go to the store to get some last-minute items. I'd just put the girls to sleep when I heard shooting outside the house. I heard multiple bullets fired at once, and so, being a Pentecostal, I immediately got on my knees and started praying. I believed this somehow would stop the violence. (As you can see, I hadn't changed that much from what that pastor was doing by stretching hands toward the east.)

The shots continued to ring out, and I started praying harder and harder and harder. It literally sounded like World War III was happening right outside my front door. I lifted my head, genuinely curious how anyone could maintain this level of violence for such an extended period. I got up, cracked open the door a bit, and realized I wasn't in World War III. The Oakland As had just won a baseball game. And that "gunfire" I heard? It was celebratory fireworks popping off.

That was a real "come to Jesus" moment for me. My bias was standing out in bold effect. I was carrying around a lot of fear, and I was driven by my perception of what might happen while living in "that kind of neighborhood"—rather than waiting to experience what actually *did* happen.

Get to Know Your Neighbor

After just a few months of living there, I became accountable to my mission and began doing community work in West and East Oakland. It was then that I learned the history of the area from sisters who kept inviting me to their homes for a cup of coffee.

The older women of the neighborhood told me that West Oakland was really the first thriving community for Black people on the West Coast. They told the stories of how their parents, escaping the horrors and lynchings and discrimination and domestic terrorism of Jim Crow, got on the train leaving the South and took it to the end of the train line, which was at the West Oakland Southern Pacific Depot. They were trying to get as far away from white supremacy as they could. At this last stop in California, their parents and other migrants in the Great Migration found a thriving community with Black-owned businesses, jazz clubs, and restaurants, and Seventh Street became a cultural hub.

In the late 1940s, the public transit electric streetcar was shut down by GM, leaving those without cars stranded and estranged from opportunities to get to work. The 1950s brought an intensified racial divide, a housing crisis, and redlining, in which mortgage brokers, bankers, and others refused to lend and provide services to people in certain neighborhoods deemed "too risky" for investment. In the 1970s, all the manufacturing plants in West Oakland were shut down, and the people who had jobs within walking distance from their homes no longer had a place to work. All of this caused the neighborhood to go into a deep dive. That's when crime, drugs, and addiction began to infiltrate. Federal intervention and "urban renewal"—including claiming eminent domain over a part of that cultural hub at Seventh Street to build out a new transit line—kept Black folks crowded in one section of the city. These actions created blight and slums.

My neighbors shared with me that while others focused on the violence that broke out in our community, no one was focusing on the criminality of the conditions placed on these newly arrived migrants from the Jim Crow South. No one was unearthing that the Oakland Police Department, like many other California police departments, began recruiting white, racist police officers from Mississippi and Alabama to come to California to help police their "Negro problem." Instead of criminalizing the policies and practices that led to the conditions, society criminalized the people, putting them in a worse condition.

Over many cups of coffee and long afternoons in parlors still intact, these community historians spoke to me of the intrusive and exclusive dynamics that literally destroyed their neighborhood. My neighbors weren't in this current condition because of the choices they made or because they lacked personal responsibility or because they failed to work hard. They were the victims of decades-old, ripple-effect choices made by other people with power and privilege—people who did not see Black folks as belonging in their circle of human concern.

This deeper understanding of their experiences helped me better manage my bias. My bias was still there, but it didn't control me in the same way as it had when I didn't have these insights from real people from the neighborhood.

Our past tries to hold us hostage. Our past wants us to make meaning of our present by using things that have happened previously as points of reference. Our past shapes the way we see the world. It gives us an ability to see certain people and certain stories, but it also hampers our ability to see them for more than what we perceive them to be. We cling instead to the stories we've created about them in our minds. I learned this again and again during my years living in the Kill Zone.

Yet even with all I learned and all that I knew, when these young brothers from the Kill Zone shared their stories with me—stories about serious issues within a police force that was known to be problematic and that had been under federal investigation for many years—I still didn't believe them. I let my bias, based on my experiences and my perceptions from my past, get the best of me.

The young men knew I did not believe them. But that did not cause them to abandon me or the process. They were still building shared humanity with me. They were still offering me a level of generosity and grace that, frankly, my actions demonstrated I did not deserve. They were already wanting and ready to build, while I, the teacher, was still learning how.

Owning Your Mistakes

My delay in believing the young men led to a pivotal moment in my journey of becoming. Years later, I found out they were, indeed, telling the truth. Numerous media outlets began confirming their stories about the police department. As the *Baltimore Sun* reported in September 2015, "A suicide note left by an Oakland police officer suggested he had been engaged in a sexual relationship with a young sex worker in the city's troubled Fruitvale neighborhood, which includes International Boulevard, Oakland's main prostitution stroll. The investigation widened in the summer, when Jasmine, then publicly known by another name, told a television reporter that she had sex with more than a dozen members of the Oakland Police Department as well as officials with other law enforcement agencies in Alameda and Contra Costa counties."

A 252-page internal affairs document released in 2019 reportedly showed "explicit and salacious details, including graphic messages [that] reveal the relationship between officers and a teenage girl named Jasmine, who went by the name 'Celeste Guap'" at the time. The document also showed that a sergeant in the police department knew about this misconduct and failed to stop it or to report it. That failure to report is a violation of police policy. Jasmine, who has now spoken publicly about the scandal, also revealed that officers gave her inside information about police raids. Several of the officers faced criminal charges, and many were fired. In 2017, the city settled a civil suit and paid Jasmine $980,000.

Unfortunately, by the time news of the scandal broke, I wasn't able to go back to the young men who had confided in me about the exploits of the Oakland Police Department. I couldn't even remember their names. I remember their faces and their stories but not their names. This still causes me embarrassment and deep pain. I couldn't even remember the very people I had relocated my family to East Oakland to advocate for, those who had offered me truth and trust that I, at the time, refused to believe. Self-awareness can be a hard pill to swallow.

Without the opportunity to do restorative healing with the specific young men, I decided to speak more openly with other young brothers who were impacted by violence. I couldn't repair the specific harm of not having believed specific men, but I could own my failures of the past and make a choice to tell this story more publicly.

These days, I tell the story not as a badge but as a sacred practice of public repentance. I feel a deep sense of responsibility to ensure that I tell the truth about a time I missed the mark in a really big way—one that mattered. This is the ugly truth: I, Ben McBride, with all my awareness and education and commitment, was still being ruled by my implicit bias in the face of the very people I was seeking to serve. I was trying to confront the empire, and in many ways I was confronting the empire yet was still struggling with, as Bishop T. D. Jakes says, the enemy "in-a-me."

If we're unaware of our implicit bias, then we're unaware of how limited we are. We won't be able to create tables where true bridging and belonging happen because our implicit bias tells us stories about who belongs at that table and the value they bring or lack. We will begin to eliminate certain people from the table, which reduces our circle of human concern, our ability to be open to one another.

Here is an implicit bias activity that you can utilize to become more aware of your biases during everyday interactions. I teach this technique to individuals in communities and within organizations and corporations around the world. You can apply it to various areas of your life.

Write down the names of the ten people you spend the most time around, listing them from one to ten in a column on the left side of the paper. After you list the ten people you spend the most time around, add six more columns with headers: race, gender, age, religion, sexual orientation, and political identity. Then, taking each name, fill out each row so you have a profile of each person. And then look for the similarities that exist in the people you spend the most time around. Think about who *isn't* among the people you spend your most time around. Which groups of people aren't found on your list? Looking at this list can potentially help you identify some of your biases. People to whom we do not have social proximity are the people we end up making assumptions about. We are more at risk of being influenced by unhealthy meta-narratives about people we never interact with.

While we can't change the obstruction spots we have in a small amount of time (if ever), we can be aware of them. And with this awareness, we can ask ourselves: Am I really seeing, hearing, feeling what I think I'm seeing and hearing? Or might I be making assumptions because of the biases I carry? It's this practice that, in essence, helps us be better drivers than the distracted minivan driver whom the cyclist talked about in that public safety meeting. We need to double check not just our mirrors but also look over our shoulder to ensure we don't accidentally run somebody down.

So we've got to push ourselves, as leaders and regular folks, to be real about having biases, and we need to be formed by new experiences, stories, and encounters. Difference is a necessary fuel to create new outcomes. Only when we push ourselves will we be able to truly expand the circle of human concern.

5

Expand the Circle

The only time I've had a gun pointed at me was when I was eighteen years old. I was a college student working nights as a security guard at a corporate office on Sansome Street in downtown San Francisco, in the financial district, to pay my way through junior college. That night, I was leaving my swing shift and was eager to get home. I had decided to take off my security uniform before heading out. So I put on my Shaquille O'Neal Orlando Magic jersey, changed out of my black clunky security boots, slid into my sweet Ellesse tennis shoes, and threw on my Oakland Raiders parka.

As I was crossing 3rd and Market Street at about 10:30 p.m., I noticed a car driving close behind me. It was late, and the downtown was fairly deserted, so there was no reason for this car to drive so slowly. I crossed the street and kept walking. I looked behind me once and then again. The car was still there. I thought somebody was about to try to rob me, and without many people around, I wasn't sure what I would do to protect myself.

Suddenly I noticed another car speeding against traffic, down a one-way street, toward me. The car turned right in my direction. I thought it was going to run me over, so I jumped back against the wall of a building—and that's when the blinding lights hit me.

I heard people jumping out of a car and someone screaming, "Get your hands up! *Get your fucking hands up!*" My hands shot up in the air as I realized nobody was trying to rob me.

It was law enforcement, and I was immediately scared for my life.

I stood there, frozen, thinking I might be killed if I made any kind of move. Me—a church boy who sang in the choir. Yet in that moment, at 10:30 at night on 3rd Street in San Francisco, I was just another young Black man in a basketball jersey and a puffy coat. I was doing absolutely nothing but walking down the street and existing in my own skin.

The officers approached me and demanded my ID while keeping the light in my face. It was so bright I could hardly see. Only the silhouetted images of their white faces were visible. They took my ID and told me to turn around and face the wall. They frisked me, rubbing their hands over my body, and then turned me around. They told me to stay up against the wall and not to move.

I felt tears rolling down my face. I was terrified, and I thought I was going to die. It's a horrible feeling when the people who you've been told are there to protect you single you out as the one people need to be protected from—just because of how you look. Through my tears, I could make out an older Black man who was standing about thirty feet away from me, waiting at the bus stop that I had been walking to. I looked over at him, and he motioned for me to not say anything and just be cool. He had obviously seen this type of situation before or perhaps been at the receiving end of this treatment himself. Seeing him there steadied me somehow and made me feel a little less alone. The number 15 bus arrived. He shouted over, "You taking this bus?" I nodded yes but did not speak. There I was, standing against that cold wall, waiting for what would come next. He said he would wait for me—and he did.

About five minutes later, a white officer in a plain white sweatshirt and blue jeans with a crew cut and mustache walked over to me and said, "You'll be okay. We're just waiting for a witness to be brought around." He explained there had been a robbery a couple of blocks away and that I "fit the description." On the radio, however, I overheard this same officer say, "This guy's not six-foot-six, 250 pounds . . . but we'll wait." After another ten minutes or so, another cruiser came around, and the police confirmed what they already knew: I was not the guy.

The plainclothes police officer handed me my ID and said, "You're free to go."

There was no apology, no acknowledgment of their mistake, no concern as to whether I was okay. Had they asked, they would have learned that no, I was not okay.

The police officers drove away, taking their accusatory bright light and my dignity with them. In the darkness, I walked shakily toward the bus stop, my sweet Ellesse barely making a sound against the pavement.

The next bus pulled up within a couple of minutes. I got on it and walked all the way to the back. The older Black man who had seen the whole thing and had waited for me walked to the back too. We sat down on opposite sides of the bus at window seats. I still had tears rolling down my face. We didn't say another word to each other, but we didn't have to. It was the most intimate conversation I've ever had with a stranger, who really wasn't one anymore, as we headed back toward our own community.

Before my own encounter with the police at eighteen years old, police violence had already hit my family. It had given me good reason to be so terrified that night, standing on the opposite side of an officer's gun. Like so many Black and brown families, mine has a history with the police. My father told me the story of his uncle being killed by white men, who were likely KKK members, outside of Goldsboro, North Carolina, because he had a white girlfriend. He was attacked, hit over the head, and left for dead on the train tracks, a brutal custom in the South at that time. Rumor had it that some of those men were off-duty police officers.

My dad was locked up in North Carolina when he was only thirteen years old. He was detained and arrested during a student protest against Jim Crow racism and police brutality in the South. Then my brother, Mike, was beaten by San Jose police when he was a Bible college student in Santa Cruz. He was commuting between the two towns as he took care of a pastor on dialysis. Police officers stopped and assaulted him on his way back to school.

All that trauma has stayed with me my entire life. It is a part of my story and the story of Black and brown people in

America. So I have reason to mistrust law enforcement, and I have reason to have anxiety when I have encounters with police. And I brought that trauma and mistrust and anxiety with me—within me—when I sat down at the table with law enforcement to end violence in our Oakland community more than twenty-five years later. It's hard to build shared humanity when instinct and history are whispering that you might not be safe.

What Is Shared Humanity?

One of the first Oakland Ceasefire meetings we had was in the police chief's office in downtown Oakland. I walked into the elevator, and two police officers in their blue uniforms stepped in with me. As we were going up, I started to break out into a sweat. All that trauma, mistrust, and anxiety that exist in my body are still triggered when I am in proximity to law enforcement, even when we're supposedly working on the same issues.

Many of us who worked with Ceasefire felt this type of anxiety as we sat down at the table with law enforcement during our meetings, particularly as people of color—whether based on our own experiences, the experiences of people we love, or the experiences of people around the world who look like us.

But we started to discover something interesting. While we as people of color were sitting down with our mistrust and anxiety, the police officers were also sitting down at the table with their own mistrust and anxiety. We were all carrying anxiety, albeit for different reasons.

Comparing trauma was not on any agenda, nor should it be. But when we began to recognize that we were all showing up at this table with a level of anxiety—wondering whether we'd be seen as human beings, or whether our voices would be heard, or whether our perspectives would be respected—something shifted. Strangely enough, this shared anxiety became a commonality between us, and it allowed us to build a relationship, which is a key milestone for forming a shared humanity.

What is shared humanity? It's a circle of human concern big enough to hold all our similarities and all our differences. It's a table large enough for all our suffering as well. Imagining that type of circle, that type of table, is necessary for us to create a world of radical belonging.

I acknowledge, however, that building shared humanity isn't always easy. In fact, it can get hella messy. Because when we all finally decide to take a seat at the table, that decision does not magically wipe out our bias or cancel our beefs with each other. It doesn't wipe out our fear. Being at the table tends to shine a bright light on our biases and create an environment where those biases may negatively guide our decisions, influence our reactions, and cause chasms between us and those with whom we hope to bond.

When that happens, it is critical that we don't abandon the table and give up. This discomfort is part of the process, and believe it or not, we need that drama. This drama is necessary because we need to have our comfort disrupted. Without that disruption, we run the risk of simply living out the models of hegemony and colonialism that seek to create that "false peace" Dr. King talked about. Disruption helps us move from building shared humanity to the work of bridging across difference. We will not bridge without the disruption. Rather than bridge, we run the risk of trying to dominate.

Abandoning the table isn't just counterproductive; when we walk away, it stalls the progress we'd make if we just hang in there through the discomfort. And abandoning the table—whether in private settings or public ones—doesn't only look like standing up and walking away in the midst of a disagreement. Abandoning the table happens when the head of the city council abruptly ends a meeting as soon as the community gets heated and starts asking the tough questions on the mic. Abandoning the table happens when a father yells "No!" at the dinner table and storms off. Abandoning the table happens when the director of marketing cancels an entire campaign during a presentation while the team is trying to figure it out together and make it work.

We need the intensity of these moments to shake out the very things within us that are blocking our ability to create a shared future together. This way, we can confront them with curiosity, empathy, love, and understanding rather than with anger and hostility that keep our barriers to connection firmly in place.

Imagination Required

After our first year of building the table for the Oakland Ceasefire strategy and bringing the community together, the city experienced a near 30 percent reduction in homicides. This meant that thirty-nine fewer people lost their lives than the year before. This improvement made a material difference in the lives and experiences of people in the community, and one major reason we experienced this peace was because we imagined it could happen. We genuinely believed it could happen—despite the violence that sometimes seemed insurmountable. Operating this way meant we were, as the saying goes, trying to "live our way into new ways of thinking rather than trying to think our way into new ways of living."

When we operate in this way, we set goals for ourselves based on the relief that the Persecuted and the Prevented need, and we begin to act in alignment with our imagination rather than waiting for the most ideal time to move forward. This strategy is a call for people to get to work on what must be done. We choose goals based on what must happen to widen the circle of human concern, not on what seems achievable.

Abolitionists of the 1800s didn't work toward a less odious form of enslavement; they imagined freedom. The women of the women's suffrage movement didn't ask for input into their husbands' political opinions; they imagined voting. Early on, the civil rights movement often imagined too small, as elders like Bishop Calvin Woods of Birmingham, Alabama, formerly Dr. King's driver, told me. They first worked on public accommodations and then voting rights—only to realize they needed to be working on the larger human rights of Black people to have full citizenship, without restraint. Eventually, for many of them, this included calls for the eradication of poverty and systemic racism. While working toward our goal can happen either in incremental strategies or in massive structural change, we must challenge ourselves to imagine what *should* be, not merely what *can* be.

When we are becoming and belonging and bridging and building shared humanity, our imagination has to be our driving force. We have to, as the Christian scripture says, rely on our faith, which is "the substance of things hoped for, the evidence of things not seen." This is the same level of faith that visionary leaders like Dr. Martin Luther King held on to tightly and what he encouraged other leaders of the movement to hold on to as well. It is the level of faith that allows you to imagine a world where the othered are no longer ostracized, where everyone belongs at the table, where everyone has space within the circle of human concern, and where we are consistently building shared humanity.

Building shared humanity doesn't magically change the long-term structural conditions in our society: the conditions that have created the anxiety that causes us to break. It doesn't immediately fix the othering that we have experienced. But it does help us imagine a shared future across what we have in common as well as how we differ. In order to get there, there have to be seats at the table for those who are most excluded and most impacted, as well as seats at the table for those of us who have the most anxiety.

Like I said, at some level, everyone at the table has anxiety but for different reasons. The Powerful and the Privileged often carry high anxiety because of the fear of losing power and the concern that the future doesn't have a place for them. While we can see this clearly in the US history of racism, and particularly in white men who resist the emergence of BIPOC and woman leadership, this human dynamic can show up anywhere in our organizations, in our churches, and in any system rooted in hierarchy. The

Persecuted and the Prevented carry different anxiety to the table. For them, it's more about what happens if things *don't* change. What does the status quo mean for their ability to continue to exist? How can they protect themselves from the violence the Powerful and Privileged often mete out to protect their own comfort?

As we all wrestle with anxiety—our own and that of others—we must be willing to sit at the table through what I and clergy friends I worked with in the Bay Area call *shared awkwardness*. During the initial phases of building shared humanity, a sense of shared awkwardness often permeates the room. It's one that most people instinctively want to avoid. Building shared humanity is an experience in how we're different, and we've been socialized to fear that difference. Many of us have experienced trauma that suggests difference presents a threat. These experiences of building shared humanity are ones we *need* to do. We may not *want* to do them, but we *have* to. Staying engaged in that tension long enough to discover shared aspirations for the future we want to create is critical; otherwise, we won't be able to unpack our old stories and build a new story together.

This commitment to staying engaged requires us to not only adopt a different way of thinking; it requires us to embrace a different way of being. It requires us to have a level of imagination that is forward-thinking and not trapped in our past, which is where our bias wants to keep us. And it requires us to ask different questions of ourselves.

You can build shared humanity in your everyday life— and you may already be doing so. As you live in your community and carry out your day-to-day routines, I'd like you to consider some questions rooted in imagination, that seed of shared humanity:

- What does a future in my organization, community, or family look like, and how can I serve that cause from where I am today?
- What's holding me back from dreaming big ideas for the world I want?
- Who's not at my table who needs to be there for us to widen the circle of human concern in my organization, community, or family?

Here are the ways that I address these questions in my own life when being guided by my imagination:

- I imagine a world where my great-grandchildren are no longer afraid of the police.
- I imagine a world where I'm not defined by whom I vote for but by the flourishing of my local community.
- I imagine a world where people love one another.
- I imagine a world where people are not overlooked for a job interview because of their name and can be employed for the skills and excellence they possess.
- I imagine a world where families are no longer broken by external societal pressures.

Terry Supahan, executive director of True North Organizing Network, which works on racial justice in Northern California among the tribal lands—once told me that every decision he makes is a decision that must have the next seven generations in mind. If we can begin to function in that way—with that same incredible, forward-looking imagination—then maybe we can build some shared humanity. Maybe then we can author a new, shared tomorrow.

What about you? What questions are you willing to ask yourself? What new world will you imagine?

Staying at the Table Requires Glue

When we *fail* to stay at the table, hear each other, and honor each other's unique experiences, we break. We talked about what that looks like in chapter 3. To stay at the table—to do that messy work to create a shared humanity together—we need glue to keep us there. That glue is relationships.

We are a part of each other. And as part of each other, we have to learn to hold space for each other, to be in relationship with each other. James Baldwin wrote, "Each of us, helplessly and forever, contains the other—male and female, female and male, white and Black and Black and white. We are a part of each other." Having this important awareness is where we root our process of building shared humanity.

In our work in Oakland, I had an unfavorable opinion about and history with the police. Many of the people of color I worked with did as well. We shared those experiences among us, even when we didn't speak about them. We had an unspoken relationship between us, just as I had with the older Black man on the bus.

Within the Oakland Ceasefire Steering Committee, I expected I would have a shared experience with the other faith leaders in the room, but it turned out that we did not. When we talked about spiritual leadership, we felt like we were very similar. But our differences—in generation, theology, race, and class—presented various challenges toward progress. The older Black preachers shunned some of us younger preachers for not respecting their ways and how they'd arrived at this time in our history. We younger preachers critiqued them because we thought they hadn't accomplished all we wished they had. The Pentecostals were seen as uneducated Christian radicals, while the Baptists were seen as educated and elitist. The white pastors were often quiet, trying to figure out their place—but the police and other civic leaders would always turn to them for rescue in times of tension anyway. That dynamic created resentment among the Black pastors.

Within all of that, some of us were more economically well-off and pastored churches with deep pockets, while others were grassroots faith leaders who lived paycheck to paycheck, irrespective of generation, race, or even education. So although we shared the same aspiration for reducing gun violence in our communities, we let these differences stunt our progress and even our aspirations. We sometimes became suspicious of each other's intentions because we didn't have enough understanding of each other's backgrounds and how each person made meaning. Stunted moves built on suspicion sound like this:

"Why do I need to listen to Pastor Joe? He's not out in the streets where it's at; he's up in his high-rise church."

"I don't think it's necessary to give them a leg up because if we do, they won't work hard to end this."

"You're not from this neighborhood; I am. You could never understand."

We all had to take time to challenge the suspicions we brought. We had to listen, share, and be open to others' perspectives and experiences. Even those of us who were aligned as a bloc—the ministers—had to do our work. We had relationships within relationships: ones that needed to be addressed, healed, and nurtured before we could start to do the work. We couldn't erase or disappear our identities while doing the work. We all carried our stories with us.

This process allowed us to sit again at the same table to begin to build a strategy that could work for our collective lift. Challenging this suspicion also required us to build relationships with law enforcement representatives who were also at the table. Once again, messy.

Holding space requires us to activate all the tools we use to build relationships. It's Relationships 101: we need to actively share our own perspectives and listen to the perspectives of others without judgment. We must also actively recognize our commonalities and our differences and actively see each other as part of one another. Sounds easy, but it's often hard.

Some important things to remember when sharing your own perspective:

- Be vulnerable and have courage to share your story—good, bad, and ugly.
- Have trust that your story is worthy and valid.
- Use your voice to speak up. Silence neither protects nor helps.

Here are some important things to remember when listening to the perspective of others. You might feel like you know these things already, but we can all use reminders:

- Be quiet when others are speaking.
- Remove your bias from your frame of reference to allow your heart to receive and ears to hear the other.
- Ask questions that clarify but do not accuse nor belittle or embarrass.

And here is how to recognize differences and commonalities:

- Start from a place of imagining you are more like the others in the group than different.
- Accept that people are different without judging the difference or the person.
- Share and listen to perspectives.

If you have power or privilege, what proximity do you have to the pain of others? In what ways have you moved to the center of the Quadrants so that you can have a better understanding of the Persecuted and the Prevented? Where has life placed you as the Powerful or Privileged? Or where might you have been Persecuted? Has there been a time you were among the Prevented? What is your relationship like with those who have been othered?

If you are experiencing persecution or prevention, what possibilities might open up a different future with the Powerful and the Privileged? What will you need to see to give you faith in the process? What does a healthy version of a relationship look like that doesn't cause you to become a caricature of the current power dynamics?

Seeing Each Other as Part of One Another

As part of my follow-up Ceasefire call-in sessions, I was scheduled to meet with George and Larry, two young brothers who had been identified as being "at risk to commit an act of violence or be a victim of violence."

In anticipation of their arrival at our Cityteam office, where I would be able to offer them access to resources and programs, I asked the support staff to set up our meeting room in the same way as when I would meet with influential city leaders or donors who were supporting our nonprofit organization. That meant white linen tablecloths and nice silverware with a catered meal and flower arrangements around the room.

Located on Washington Street, Cityteam was adjacent to the Oakland Main Police Station, the North County Jail, and the downtown Oakland courthouse. To me, our office was a path to hope in a concrete maze of incarceration. As I arrived at the office that night, I came up the stairs and saw the two young brothers sitting in the lobby waiting for me. They were nervous, as was often the case for young men entering this unfamiliar space. They were skeptical; sometimes they feared retaliation from parole officers if they didn't meet with me. They weren't always there on their own accord, and they weren't sure it was safe.

I greeted them warmly and then said, "Hey, come on. Let's have dinner together, but let's go over to this room."

George got up and walked over to the room I had indicated. He opened the door, saw all the fancy place settings, jumped out, and closed the door. "Oh, shit!" He looked at me. "Who's this for?"

"This is for y'all," I said.

Looking at Larry, he said, "This is for us?"

I opened the door again, held it open for them, and repeated, "This is for y'all!"

"All right," he said, suspicion still rimming his voice.

They walked in, hesitant to sit down to such an elaborate setup. They finally pulled out chairs, sat down at the table, and took in the room. I joined them. I watched them self-soothe for several minutes, rubbing their thighs and rubbing their arms. They were incredibly uncomfortable sitting in a place of honor. George and Larry and young brothers like them have been so dishonored in our larger national story that they often internalize a lower self-worth. Poor people of color are disenfranchised by racism in America. All those structural and systemic dynamics remain at play even when they step into places of honor.

By now in life, when I walk into a place of honor, I naturally feel like I belong there, but I had to build shared humanity with George and Larry to recognize that when they entered those spaces, they did not. I believed in honoring them because I knew what it felt like to be honored as a Black man and because I saw us as a part of each other. I built a table to demonstrate that. I also built a table that I hoped would help them take a few steps out of their comfort zone and let them try on a new one, even if only for a short while. I wasn't asking them to not be who they were or to *act* like somebody else. We made lots of jokes about not spilling stuff on the white tablecloth and what if the fellas could see them now. We worked on being ourselves in this environment. By the end of our dinner, they felt more comfortable in that space. Their shoulders relaxed, smiles released the tension in their foreheads, and they enjoyed themselves.

We are humanity to one another; we are humanity together. Building a shared humanity includes recognizing our bias, our anxiety, our similarities, our differences, and everything that makes us who we are. A journey of radical belonging includes building shared humanity by creating more space for experiences beyond our own, bridging across difference rather than breaking because of it, and choosing cocreation with those we are bridging with.

Building shared humanity is about creating the tables and the practices for us to share our stories—not just the stories that we articulate with words but the stories that our bodies and our hearts and our minds carry. Ensuring we build those tables in a way that they are large enough to hold everyone's suffering is critical to a world of radical belonging. But building tables is not enough. What we *do* at those tables, and how we bridge across difference, is what legitimizes the table. This is what serves as the legs that keep it stable. From this point, we can grow, evolve, and continue to become.

George and Larry needed space to continue their becoming, and so did I. We needed to learn from each other so we could work as partners. It took courage from them to come to the space I built, and it took courage for me to build it. We all have something to do for radical belonging, even though those "somethings" are not the same as someone else's.

6

Evolve Your Movement

I knew the protests of 2020 had about a ninety-day shelf life.

Don't get me wrong: I was glad to see so many people, of all different backgrounds and ages, in the streets, all around the world, rallying for Black lives. After witnessing the brutal murder of George Floyd—and far too many others—at the hands of police, we needed an uprising of that magnitude. Still, I was concerned that if we didn't build some institutional power and establish relationships with leaders in the private, public, and cultural sectors—leaders who were finally awakening to a very old problem—they would simply do some virtue signaling and then return to business as usual.

Unfortunately, that's exactly what happened. As soon as the pressure subsided, many officials and leaders moved on.

Somehow our pain and rage ended up fueling more compliance and conformity versus community and transformation.

Like many other activists, I bounced around during the height of the 2020 protests. We moved around from injustice to injustice, tragedy to tragedy. I went to Louisville, Kentucky, twice to stand with the young people in the streets and protest the police killing of Breonna Taylor in her home. I was in the streets of Oakland, where teenaged Black kids were leading protests that grew as large as ten thousand people.

We marched down Broadway, and together we relaunched a national police reform campaign called Bring the HEAT. This campaign focused on hiring, equipment, accountability, and training for law enforcement. We wanted to rid policing of the Proud Boys and other alt-right groups, demilitarize the tactics, create more citizen oversight, and invest in anti-racism work for those who serve. We became active in more than twenty states around the country as thousands took the pledge to engage their local elected officials around this shift. We went to Washington, DC, where we pushed for the George Floyd Justice in Policing Act of 2021 that banned chokeholds, and we challenged qualified immunity, which limits the rights of victims of police violence to hold officers and government officials accountable.

Yet just one year later, despite all the good work that had happened and the heightened awareness around police brutality, we couldn't get this reform accomplished, even with the Democrats in control of the House, the Senate, and the presidency. We had worked so hard to get the George Floyd Justice in Policing Act passed—a federal law that would ban chokeholds and no-knock warrants on citizens by their police departments, as well as ban racial profiling and a culture that allows police officers to break laws without accountability. Instead, we got Juneteenth as a holiday. Instead of real remedies for the material injustice that Black and brown people have experienced for generations, we got as president one of the authors of the tough-on-crime political movement of the '90s, which removed Black men from their families, homes, and communities. It was virtue signaling—and a poor version of it—at best.

The opportunity to create real change was there, but the will of the Powerful and the Privileged was not. Black people were still being killed every twenty-eight hours in this country by police, a security guard, or a vigilante. And this was *after* all the marches and the protests and the apologies from white folks and the Black Lives Matter statements of support from corporations. Things were not changing.

This was proof to me that you can know you have to do the right thing and have every intention of doing the right thing. But if you're not strategic in your approach and clear about your desired outcomes, you will accomplish nothing.

I learned this important lesson as an organizer and emancipation practitioner in Oakland. My comrades and I realized that as people who were practicing freedom and practicing peace, we had to remember that a tactic is only as relevant as its ability to achieve the strategic goals. When strategies stop working, the movement must evolve.

The evolution of a movement—and of a self—is inevitable. As the times change, we as individuals change too. Our contribution to the movement might shift as well. Even though our commitment to justice must remain unwavering, *how* we show up and in what spaces we show up may shift. We have to understand our evolving and be okay with it—even if others aren't.

Beat of a Different Drum

I first realized that my contribution to the Movement for Black Lives was evolving in 2017. I had arrived at a place of deep sadness and loneliness after realizing the extent of the struggle that existed *within* the movement. I started to encounter people who were trying to delegitimize me and the work I was doing—people I had assumed were allies. And I, admittedly, had started doing the same to others. I had fallen into the trap of othering so that I, myself, could feel safe and protected.

I realized we were losing our ability to hold more than a "single story," as author Chimamanda Ngozi so brilliantly argues in her work. All of us are vulnerable to buying into a single story, and activists are no exception. We were in danger of believing a single story that said there is no future in expanding the "we" that Brother Bob spoke of, that call-out culture is the only useful mechanism, that we in the movement were right, and that any culturally and politically conservative person had nothing valid or valuable to offer.

Eventually, after pausing, praying, and reflecting, I realized these problems were spiritual, not political. To overcome them, I would have to make a change, regardless of what anyone else thought about it.

During this time, I was inspired by the work of Sikh activist and author Valerie Kaur, who acknowledges that the future appears dark and then offers us this question: "What if this darkness is not the darkness of the tomb but the darkness of the womb?" I also was inspired by a Ugandan man who approached me when I was speaking at Hofstra University. He challenged me that the binary call I had just issued—to either be a "chaplain to this failing empire" or be a "prophet of the righteous resistance"—was insufficient. That was too simplistic, he told me. He said I needed to evolve my thinking to the invitation for us to become "midwives to the Beloved Community." The midwife isn't pregnant and yet plays a critical role in assisting the one carrying life. That life represents the next stage: the evolution.

It was in listening to others that I began to evolve. And it was not just any others but Black women, women of color, and wise ones from the motherland who invited me to embrace a spiritual approach to the movement toward belonging instead of the more linear approach.

For me, this meant I had to become fully, deeply rooted in the truth that we are all radically interconnected. None of us is disposable. It meant I would have to make room for even those possessed by the fury and rage of racism and other forms of othering. Somehow, in this turbulent historical moment, I still had to listen and offer a spiritual approach to engaging that anger rather than a retributive one. As I worked in Oakland, and statewide in California, and nationally, as my work continued to grow, I had to get comfortable being disinvited from certain tables and not making the wrong meaning of the disinvitation. I needed to see the disinvitation as a "not yet" or a "not me" instead of "let me center my angst again and turn up even harder."

This has been a struggle for me. When I'm triggered to turn up, I have to remember that holding on to the spirituality behind the work is critical. It's the work I feel I must do and that I must call others to do.

This recalibrated approach is more spiritual than political. We'll look at its contours in this chapter. But it's important to note here that as we evolve, how we measure impact begins to change as well. I'm now measuring less often with numbers (How many people did we convince to come to the table?) and more often qualitatively (How are we all becoming?). And this measurement starts with me. Am I healthier as I participate in the movement? Am I hurting myself and others less often? Am I more open to different perspectives that trigger me? Am I more willing to build tables larger than my quadrant and bridge across difference when I sit there? Am I willing to cocreate for the world we deserve instead of the world I think I can "organize" to get? Are others moving in this way?

Those living in the future, I believe, will judge our impact; we can't do that yet. Dr. Martin Luther King was said to be disliked by the majority of his own tribe, the National Baptist Convention, during his leadership. Yet just as he said when quoting French author Victor Hugo during his speech to North Carolina students who sat in protest at a lunch counter at F. W. Woolworth in 1960, "There is nothing in all the world more powerful than an idea whose time had come."

Shift Your Perspective

As painful as it has been when someone called me on my shit, I am grateful. I've had many such moments throughout my twenty-plus years as an activist and a leader in the movement for radical belonging. These moments cause me to pause and reconsider the issue at hand, but they also often make me shift my perspective completely—and in a way that centers the Persecuted and Prevented instead of my own objectives or the change *I* think is needed. And usually it is someone within the Persecuted and Prevented quadrants who brings about this shift.

After one of our call-in sessions in Oakland, I spoke with one of the young brothers who was a participant in the gun violence plaguing our city. He and I had stepped outside the building, and as we were saying goodbye, I told him, in no uncertain terms, "We need you to put the guns down. That's the only reason why we're bringing y'all to these tables and having these conversations: because you matter and because I want you to live to be as old as I am. I need you to put the gun down."

This young man, who was about thirty years old at the time, challenged me in a way no one else had ever challenged me. "Ben, you're telling me to put the gun down," he said. "But are you asking me to put the gun down for me or for *you*?" I stood there, speechless.

He went on. "You need to understand that for me, that gun on the corner is what creates the sense of belonging for me. That gun is what creates a sense of safety for me. That gun—because people know *I* am the one who'll pull that trigger—is the thing that ensures I can walk around, and people who are connected to me can walk around, and have some sense of safety."

He paused for a moment, letting his comment sink in. "So if I put the gun down, that means I lose the space and the role I have in the clique that I belong to," he continued. "When I put the gun down, that means I've got to live with a different level of stress and anxiety." He pointed his finger at me and said, "Then y'all don't want me to smoke weed either because I got a pee test with the probation officer. And so you want me to walk around with all that anxiety, and I can't smoke weed, and I've got to be worried about my safety."

I sat down on a nearby bench.

"I've seen you on Facebook," he said, holding out his cell phone for me to look at the photographs on my Facebook page. "You're sitting there, and you're all 'cupcaking' with your wife, and y'all got your little pictures with you and your family and your kids and all of that." He sat down next to me, looked at me, and asked pointedly, "When I put the gun down, am I coming to your house for the holiday? If I put the gun down, am I gonna come over to 'cupcake' with you and your family?" I didn't respond. I had no idea what to say.

"So let's just be clear: when you're asking me to put the gun down, are you asking me to put the gun down for *me*? Or are you asking me to put the gun down for *you*?"

I had no answer. No argument. I was stumped. When I'd made the request for him to put his gun down, I had hoped—actually, I had honestly expected—that he would say, "Okay, Ben. I'll do it."

But this brother saw our differences and wanted to make sure I was seeing them too. He saw and named the conditions of his life in a way I could not ignore. I had to sit in the tension of that moment, and listen, and take it all in, no matter how uncomfortable it made me. Because his perspective was the future of what we were trying to create.

Eyes Wide Open

Reducing gun violence required me to think about solving the issue in a way that wasn't just about creating safety for *me*; it was ultimately about creating belonging for *him* and for all the people who were most impacted by the violence themselves. I had to evolve my thinking. My view now is that we need a massive movement of bridging and belonging, with strategies targeted at—and crafted by—the people who don't see themselves in the future.

Some white people don't yet see themselves in a more pluralistic version of the United States in the future, where they are led by BIPOC. As I've sat with some of these white people, I've heard from them that they don't know how to belong outside of where their ancestors placed them: in control. They have so imbibed one version of this country's story that they don't know who they are apart from it. Some of that is bad history, and some of it is white fragility. Some of it is fear that BIPOC folks will eventually do to white people what their white ancestors—and too many living people—have done and do to them.

I also have had countless conversations with young brothers who believed there was no belonging for them in the future. They had made their peace with the idea of dying a violent death before they turned twenty-five, and they were actively participating in bringing about their own demise. They would rather cling to what they know, violently, than leave it behind for the fear of what could be.

When people don't see themselves as a part of the future, they irrationally fight to hold on to their present. That might mean even burn down the house while they're inside it. This might be difficult for many of us to imagine, but this thinking can go across race and across class. But we have to figure out how we can get some credible messengers—such as those who have already sojourned from the far corner of their quadrant—who can bear witness that it's safe. We need anyone, actually, who is empowered with empathy and compassion to assist people into a braver, safer way of being human. People who are willing to call in instead of call out.

And then we have to have some elected officials and institutional leaders making decisions differently to ensure structures aren't engendering marginality. We need them to be credible messengers to constituents who aren't aware of the impact of the status quo. Black Power activist from the 1960s Kwame Toure (formerly known as Stokely Carmichael) said when speaking about racism, "If a white man wants to lynch me, that's his problem. If he's got the power to lynch me, that's my problem. Racism is not a question of attitude; it's a question of power." In any scenario where othering is present, there will always be a need for leadership to leverage unpopular decision-making while we continually work toward a wider circle.

We also need people who are doing the cultural work of helping people imagine both themselves and the people they other in a shared future. We need those who are working on the structural conditions to be in relationship with those who are doing the cultural work of helping people understand the ever-changing ecosystem around them. Culture and structure go hand in hand. When we rush to address structural concerns alone, we will miss the mark. We have to go slow to go fast.

Hopeful examples of cultural work and structural work being paired together do exist. Undivided in Ohio, a bridging project led by a Black pastor and a white pastor and community organizer, models how we can invite people on the road of culture change in ways that have connections to structural change. In Florida, two formerly incarcerated men, Desmond Meade and Neil Volz, of Florida Rights Restoration, have conversations with Black and white communities (cultural work) around justice and mercy to restore the right to vote for all formerly incarcerated Floridians (structural work).

Simply put, failure to evolve in these ways leaves us with the whites blaming the Blacks, the Blacks blaming the immigrants, the immigrants blaming the Blacks, the Blacks internalizing the blame and blaming other Blacks. In the end, the most marginalized group ends up in a worse condition than where they began.

The Powerful and the Privileged must be held more accountable for the world we're trying to create. They have to give up the world they're trying to preserve in order to retain their power and their sense of safety. Safety is the right of all human beings, not a privileged few. Those who pick up guns and turn to violence often do so because they do not feel safe, not because they are inherently violent.

We also have to look beyond punitive measures when people do turn to violence because punitive measures don't get us to where we need to be. When I think about the shooters I worked with in Oakland, like the brother who schooled me on my limited understanding of his world, I realized they were not deterred or swayed by punitive outcomes. The threat of jail did not make them stop killing each other. The threat of losing their ability to make money? That didn't do it either. Because at the core, the reason they were engaged in that life was because of a whole consciousness that informed why they were standing on 76th and Bancroft, waiting for something to pop off and ready if it did. And until you understand that consciousness—unless you reckon with the notion that they're defending something way bigger than going to jail or something that is affecting their money on the streets or their ability to get a job—you will never make progress.

For our work in Oakland, this understanding meant finding a way to expand our own circle of human concern enough that these young men knew they belonged. We had to evolve from our demands—"stop the violence" and "put down the guns"—to a much more empathetic message. A message that said, "We see you, we hear you, we love you, we accept you, and you belong here." We had to install a strategy that was not about taking something away from them. We had to let them know we wanted *more* for them.

To be clear, we also had to have empathy and hold space for the mothers who had lost their kids to violence. Those traumatized, grieving mothers often did not want these brothers in the circle. In fact, with a few exceptions, they told me to "throw the motherfuckers underneath the jail." Those mothers didn't want them in the circle.

But expanding the circle—a circle that could hold all their suffering as well as the suffering of the young men causing this violence—was imperative for the movement. We had to sit in that tension, together.

What White Folks Can Do

Another shift I believe we need in the movement for racial justice in the United States is to activate people who are willing to go back into their own spaces and challenge the othering they witness head-on. I don't think Black folks need to try to engage alt-right groups or attempt to dry white tears. But I *do* think white people who are proximate to other white folks who occupy these spaces need to bridge with them. That's right, my white brothers and sisters: it's on *you*!

How about you try to bridge at your house, across your dinner table, across the street to your neighbor, across the pew at church? To do so, you've got to become a white person who courageously engages around the notions of race and does more than say, "Pray for Buffalo." That doesn't widen the circle. What we need you to do is have a heightened sense of awareness about the dangerous othering that is taking place around you. The murder of innocent Black folks in Buffalo—who were targeted and killed *because* they were Black—happened on your watch. You have to get good at being able to recognize when your children are being radicalized by the alt-right, white supremacist imperialism. You have to face this head-on and address this now.

While it's nice to have you stand with us—whether that's in the streets or on social media—it's crucial to have you stand up for us even when we're not there. And even when it may cause you some pain.

Don't Sell Out. Stand Up.

I have been called a sellout more times than I'd like to remember. And every time, even to this day, it breaks my heart.

I've had to deal with that label for many years. Even as I was protesting on the streets of Ferguson in 2014, I would come home to Oakland and train police departments on how to improve the relationship between themselves and the community. That was a choice I made in service to the movement of radical belonging.

Of *course* I wanted to go tell off the police like every other Black person I knew wanted to. Given what we were seeing police do in Ferguson and Baton Rouge and Minneapolis and Louisville and so many other places in America, I longed to tell them where to go—and how fast to get there. But I decided, *I'm actually going to make a different choice.* I thought to myself, *I can do that. I can choose to try to see some of their humanity, even though I'm not confident they're actually seeing mine.* I was going to challenge the racism in policing when I was engaged in my frontline work, and I was going to try to invite folks into the circle of human concern when I did my bridging work.

But from the vantage point of the police, I was too close to the protest movement. And for the protest movement, I was too close to the police. Both were at times suspicious of the work I was doing. I began to call what I was doing "occupying the radical middle." The radical middle is not the same thing as "moderate" or "independent." It isn't reached by compromise or giving in to injustice. The radical middle is the space where we hold different identities without breaking.

At times, I fell into the temptation of overcompensating: sometimes toward one side, sometimes toward the other. I'd find myself trying to virtue signal to one or the other that I'm still "about that life." So being in that bridging space has been difficult to navigate.

I have an intimate understanding of the concept of "selling out" because, I think, it has such deep roots in Black consciousness. The worst thing you can do to us is sell out! I've come to realize over time that sometimes the loudest voices belong to the people who have the most to lose from somebody threatening the status quo. In the movement, we are tainted with the same systemic issues that society is tainted with. Even among those who advocate for a world of justice, where we're all treated as equals, there are the Powerful, Privileged, Persecuted, and Prevented. Remember, the Powerful are the people who set the conditions for how things are. The Privileged are those who benefit from those conditions.

Those dynamics can happen even within movements for change. Post-Ferguson, a certain kind of consciousness arose: that certain people were leaders of the Movement for Black Lives, and some were not. Many of those "knighted" for leadership had previous history with philanthropy and connections to elected officials. Unfortunately, many of the grassroots leaders who launched the movement—mostly poor Black young people from St. Louis—were still relegated to the Persecuted and Prevented quadrants. When President Obama's White House issued invitations to Ferguson leaders to come, they didn't invite actual leaders from Ferguson; they invited those with national platforms. It was only because some of the invited leaders recused themselves in order to make room for an actual Ferguson leader that the real leaders were able to share space in the Oval Office. Although this was a nice gesture, as time went on, decisions for resources and authorship of the movement still centered the Privileged leaders, who were already proximate to the Powerful. Meanwhile, a bit like what happens in society writ large, the Persecuted and Prevented were still often left on the outside, likely having solutions they were never able to present or express. It's another example of changing everything and changing nothing.

That's why I've decided to stand up in a different way. And we each have to decide that for ourselves as we grow and evolve. You might get called a sellout. But switching up your style is not the same as selling out.

At the core of my work now is a mass movement of people, like you, who are willing to respond to the invitation to engage in the bridging and belonging work that has to happen if we are to have any future, particularly in the United States. I don't believe we will survive without it, which is why I have committed my life to it.

Keep Growing

Sometimes, as an activist, I have wondered whether the radical belonging we are longing for and working toward is, in the Christian faith, what we call heaven. I'm always challenged by the notion of whether a world of radical belonging can ever be. Can people actually find a way to exist as a community without violence and othering? Or is it a pie-in-the-sky notion that even future generations will never see? Sometimes just the question itself is overwhelming to me.

But what keeps me motivated are the little sparks—or thumbprints, as I like to call them. Over the years of our work, there's a residue left—some little thumbprints that indicate we've made some mark, had some impact. Even as we evolve slowly, as people who are on a journey to becoming, the work we are doing unfolds slowly. Thumbprints of change here and there indicate we can get there a little bit at a time.

I'm also inspired by the recognition that at a certain point in our country's history, the idea of Black folks *not* being enslaved was thought to be implausible. What a very strange, impossible, idealistic notion it must have seemed: that Black people would actually be free! For hundreds of years, Black people were property, and so individuals had no experience of anything different. I am in awe of the imagination of enslaved Africans and abolitionists to actually see a world that no one had any proof could even exist. And to say so while they were living in the midst of such violence and brutality, whether they were a victim of that violence and brutality or a witness to it. Without technology, without social media, without hashtags, without news coverage and cameras, they imagined it possible. Out of that imagination, someone said, "No. There's another world we have not reached yet, and I see it, and I'm going to work toward it. I'm going to bridge with my white abolitionists. I'm going to call them to do it. They're going to start following our leadership." And they did it.

They did it then. Imagine what we could do now. Imagine how we could set up future generations for a world of radical belonging.

That's where I find my energy to keep doing this work of imagining, and reimagining, what's possible. I hold on to the notion my ancestors had: that there has to be another version of us being people together. It might be a hundred years down the road. It might look very different than it does now. But it's important that each of us steps up and plays our role in it, even if we don't see the fruits of our labor during our lifetimes.

It's not a coincidence that we still feel so connected today to Frederick Douglass's words: "Power concedes nothing without a demand." He was saying something two hundred years ago that still frames the way we think about what needs to happen today. We're still being inspired by Mother Harriet's determination. As she led enslaved people to freedom, Harriet Tubman essentially said, "This is the work I'm going to do, and no one can stop me. Not only am I going to escape the oppression of the South, but I'm going to keep coming back into it voluntarily. I'm going to be the person who ushers people through to freedom—even though it means risking my own life in the process."

The people of the civil rights movement followed a similar call. While it looked different then than it does now, and while the tactics of nonviolence and passive resistance are still debated in some circles today, the mission was to make demands of the Powerful and the Privileged—and to do it with the knowledge that you were putting your life on the line.

The Cost of Comfort

A part of my journey has been learning where and when our ancestors made choices to trouble the waters of their generations. Our organization, Empower Initiative, leads

even death. And yet in the face of this threat, they committed themselves to actually becoming the manifestation of peace.

Another storyteller who shares with our groups, Jesse, tells us that during these protests, as a young boy, he climbed up a tree in the park to escape the ravenous German Shepherd dogs that Birmingham police officers were using to chase down the children. He climbed onto the limb of a tree in the park, wrapping his arms and legs around the strong branch. Below him stood a white police officer, with his dog biting into the air, who screamed at him, "Hey, nigger, come down and feed my dog!" In this terrifying moment, a young Jesse prayed a prayer that still rocks my soul whenever I remember this seventy-five-year-old Black man telling the story over fifty years later: "Dear Lord, please don't let this branch break. Dear Lord, please don't let this branch break."

These children of the civil rights movement demonstrated something very powerful for those of us who seek to trouble the water and lean into the urgent work of radical belonging. They teach us that the world we deserve will cost us our comfort and the opportunity to remain on the sidelines. They teach us that changing our world—whether that's within our families, the places we work, the communities we live in, or our nation as a whole—means responding to the call of our moment and being willing to put our power and privilege on the line. They teach us that as we delve deeper into the work of radical belonging, we also have help. We have each other; there is power in us doing this work together. And we even have the support of nonhuman relatives. As a young boy, Jesse found help and refuge and safety from the tree, which offered its limb to shield him from the ravenous violence of the racism below. We can do this, and we must do this. Like Jesse and Rev. Gwen and the five thousand children and young people there that day, we must trouble the water.

The work many of us are doing today is figuring out how to pick up where our elders of the last big movement left off. How do we keep widening the circle of human concern, the work they started, and build a shared humanity for our generation? And how do we remain committed to the work even though it will likely be our children or grandchildren who will fully benefit? How do we provide strong roots and dependable limbs for them to hang onto, just as that tree did for Jesse? They will likely be the first generations who can step into seeing the world that we've all deserved for the last four hundred years.

While the future we aspire to share does live in some level of imagination, we all have experienced some form of belonging in our lives. It is not as foreign to us as we might think. I know some people have very unique and difficult circumstances. But I encourage you to think back to when the first time was that you felt like you belonged. What happened in that space? Why did you feel like you belonged? And what was it about that space that made you feel you could show up as an authentic version of yourself?

We know how to live in cocreation. We know how to bridge differences. We've just been socialized to think that we get safety by segregating ourselves from people who are different and by clinging to power.

Think about young children playing in a sandbox: they practice belonging. You don't have to teach children that.

They practice it naturally. They share toys. Sure, sometimes they take toys from each other and are selfish, but we are wired, as humans, to engage with one another. Even science says that when we share with one another, when we are generous with one another, our bodies respond in a healthier way. So this call to create a world of radical belonging is not so much about what we need to learn; it is more about what we need to remember.

The call to radical belonging is a lot about *un*learning destructive behaviors and ideas. How do I unlearn this notion that because you're different from me, you are a threat? How do you? Although we might have some troubled history with one another, it doesn't make either of us threats to one another. It actually presents for us an opportunity to get curious—infectiously curious—about one another. We need to learn one another's stories. I'm a firm believer that if we don't have a common language and if we don't have a common history, there's no way to have a collective future. So we have to get curious about one another, come to know one another, so that we can recreate this kind of meta-world where that sense of belonging we knew as toddlers, as children in the sandbox, is the world we inhabit. Whether it's where we work or it's within our public systems and structures, we can create a world where we get to show up as ourselves: without violence, without othering.

Dream a New Dream

I believe in our humanity. I believe we can change the conditions so that we, as human beings, can show up in our better humanity. It's going to take a long time. We know this. But as we've said before, this is a dream you're daring to have, a work you're committing to do, for your grandchildren and great-grandchildren. We have to take ourselves and our immediate benefit out of this equation. We must become the kind of people who are thinking into the future, and we must start engaging with each other differently now. For human beings one hundred years from now to engage with each other in a more humane way, there needs to be a planet for those human beings to live on. This work is critical for our planet, and the time for us to change the way we are toward one another—to dream this new dream—is now.

The only way we will get to a world of radical belonging is if we deconstruct the one we have. Those who are the Powerful and the Privileged along any vector are going to have to be willing to deconstruct the world that has been. Deconstruction doesn't happen just for the sake of itself; we deconstruct in order to build a new foundation. And as I've shared, this work is not just for the Powerful and Privileged. This is for all of us.

We have to figure out how to rebuild this plane while it's in the sky. None of us can really stomach the plane crashing to the ground. As much as we like our intellectual critiques of hyper-capitalism—an extreme free-market system that abandons values and commodifies people, and the planet, and so on—we are also sick with the same diseases we're trying to cure. On the one hand, we're saying, "Yeah, I want this to go away." On the other hand, we're saying, "But I still need to be able to make this paper."

Many of us are trying to figure out how to create generational wealth for our relatives and loved ones because we've never had it. Some of us, as Black and brown folks, are first-generation homebuyers—unlike some of our white counterparts, who are passing down properties (in some cases, multiple properties) to their kids. So while movements take imagination, we also have to be realistic about where people are in their lives. Then we need to determine how we can help them evolve their opinions and invite them to the table.

As we each grow and gain more self-awareness about where we are within the quadrants of the Powerful, Privileged, Persecuted, and Prevented, we can be more honest with ourselves on how we're contributing to—or complicating—the movement for radical belonging. Are you the soccer mom in the minivan with good intentions who ends up being dangerous to those around her? Or are you being intentional about who you are becoming and your impact on those you set out to help? How you live now determines the story told about you in the future. What do you want generations to come to say about you?

7

Prioritize Radical Self-Care

As important as the movement for radical belonging is, so, too, is the need for radical self-care. Movement work requires you to be wholly committed to healthy practices, healthy boundaries, and a healthy amount of space to reflect, recalibrate, grieve, and heal when you need to.

This is true for all of us as human beings but especially true for those of us engaged in the work of bridging and belonging. When you are part of the Persecuted or Prevented groups working to widen the circle of human concern, it takes a toll on you. You're often working for others—advocating for them and helping them and trying to alter systems that harm them—but you must not forget that those same dynamics are impacting *you*. Every day we bump up against policies designed to harm us and people who don't accept us. We interact with those who work actively to other and oppress us and those who are in the Persecuted and Prevented quadrants. There is no way to sustain the movement, or yourself, in the face of this reality if you're not taking care of yourself. And I'm not talking about a trip to the spa or a day off—although those can be helpful too. You've got to be intentional and disciplined about this. Otherwise, this work—as powerful as it is, as well meaning as your intentions are, and as good as you want the outcome to be—could do you in bad. Real bad. I came to this realization after reaching my own breaking point.

In the summer of 2016, more and more details about the sex scandal at the Oakland Police Department were surfacing. Due to my building and bridging work, which meant often serving as a mediator between the community and the police, I found myself in the eye of the storm. Tensions were extremely high, and the moment called for a leader, someone to take some ownership of the shitstorm that was brewing.

In some ways, the sex scandal simply blew the lid off the pressure cooker that had been percolating since 2002, when the Oakland police were placed under federal oversight for other issues within the department. I, like many, was enraged. I was fighting to destroy the cultural and structural norms that had built up for so long as to allow the violence we'd all experienced. I was ready to tear that system down. I was also angry at myself for being complicit, for having tried to collaborate for too long, for not rising up against this scandal sooner. But now? Now enough was enough.

I organized a protest in which the citizens of Oakland could take to the streets and express their frustrations. Yes, that protest led to me pouring blood-red paint on the doorstep of the Oakland Police Department. And yes, I yelled at them. "Repent!" I shouted. "We charge you as guilty. Guilty of murder. We charge you as guilty of being human traffickers. We charge you as guilty for acting like peacemakers when you've been operating like terrorists." Yes, I led a march of three thousand people, who blocked traffic on both sides of the I-880 freeway, to protest police brutality and corruption and violence.

And yes, throughout it all, I was scared. Was I prepared with a step-by-step action plan? No. All I knew was that bridging had failed, trust had been broken, and belonging—the radical kind—was a crucial next step that needed to happen. All I knew was that sometimes you have to trouble the water—to disturb the thing that looks like peace on the surface but is just injustice in disguise. So I jumped into action and got determined to plan our next steps along the way. The protest was one of the ways to create space for those who didn't feel like they were heard, like they belonged, like they mattered. If we didn't do something, I feared our city would succumb to more violence. So I had to do something, and this protest was that something.

I couldn't have predicted, however, what would come next.

The Aftershock

The night after the I-880 shutdown, our group of organizers was high on adrenaline and excitement. We knew we had done something so powerful and courageous despite the fear, nervousness, and anxiety we had all experienced every moment of that night. Bravado can be overrated—it's okay to admit we're scared even as we're raising our fists for something that is right, something that makes us more human. We felt energized, focused, and eager to figure out what we could do next.

But my raised fists and loud voice that night would soon bring about a different kind of energy from outside our group. Within just twenty-four hours, I became the target of an unbelievable number of death threats and amount of online harassment.

Just three days after that march, on a Sunday, I had an already scheduled speaking engagement at a local church. I'd planned my sermon around the Good Samaritan story—about what it means to stop what you are doing, set aside your own agenda, and pay attention to someone who has been victimized along the road. The backlash from the I-880 march was so strong that someone called that predominantly white church where I was scheduled to speak and told them, "All we are telling you is you better not let that nigger stand up there Sunday."

When this report made it back to me, a swirl of questions filled my mind: Had I gone too far? Had I put my family—my wife and teenage daughters—in danger? What was I doing?

Despite my fear, I still showed up, and I still delivered my sermon that Sunday. This church, unlike a lot of white churches, was very progressive and led by LGBTQ+ folks. They had reconstructed their congregation to be led by the Persecuted and Prevented. They were used to dealing with nasty phone calls and threats.

But still, I was terrified, and I took precautions. I had my parents meet my wife, Gynelle, and me at the church that morning and take our daughters to our family church in Berkeley, just in case something happened outside of my control. I wanted Gynelle to go with them too, but she refused. She stayed with me at the church where I was speaking and sat beside me the entire time until I got up to preach. A brother from the movement I was mentoring showed up to be my eyes and ears in the lobby. I needed someone I knew would have my back. I explained the situation to him and asked him to show up. He did.

While the music played during the praise and worship time, I looked over my shoulders repeatedly. Interestingly, the faces of white men in the crowd took on a particular focus for me that day. *Could he be the one?* I wondered. *Or him?* There was a bald white man who reminded me of the man who shot Congresswoman Gabby Giffords and killed six people in 2011, and I couldn't help but check on where he was seated. This was also just one year after the massacre of nine Black churchgoers at Emanuel African Methodist Episcopal Church in Charleston, South Carolina, when a nineteen-year-old white supremacist sat in Bible study with them and then opened fire. So being in the sanctuary of a church meant nothing to me as far as the threat was concerned. Given the history of assassinated Black ministers, targeted Black Bible studies, and bombed Black churches, I knew being in a church didn't make me safe.

I took a measure of comfort in the fact that the news media had set up in the rear of the sanctuary to capture video for the evening news. I thought their presence perhaps would be a deterrent to any violence. When I stood up to speak, the assassination of Minister Malcolm X at the Audubon Ballroom played in my mind. But I took a deep breath and proceeded to offer my words despite the palpable fear.

Then within that next week, the police were threatening to arrest me for defacing public property. A Black officer on the command staff for the Oakland Police Department called me, asked me where I was, and warned me, "Stay put. Do *not* be out in public because there is a debate going on right now about arresting you. I was sitting in the room, and these white officers were banging on the table in a conversation with the chief, saying, 'Let us go get him, Chief! Say the word!'"

He told me, "Man, I said to them, 'What's wrong with y'all? This sounds like a Klan rally! What are you talking about? Don't do this.'"

His revelation terrified me to my core because of my past experiences with the police. Even though I'd worked with them in a partnership for the greater good throughout my years as an activist, that relationship was still rife with friction. In this instance, I wasn't seen as a partner. I wasn't even seen as a critic, calling for them to do better. I was seen as a threat. I was troubling the water. I was making noise—for some, too much noise.

The officer shared with me the reason I had become a threat was that I was bringing the "radicals" and the "moderates" together. When the "radicals," as he called them, protested, the police knew what to expect, and they didn't see them as much of a threat because the approach of the radicals would turn off most moderates. The radicals' harsher rhetoric, the property-damage tactics, their appearances: all this helped police win the narrative that these were people unworthy of being taken seriously.

But my work was increasingly being seen as credible by the "moderates." And for me to organize a protest where both the radicals *and* the moderates felt they belonged? That was a threat. "You brought out ministers and church ladies alongside the radicals," my contact in the department told me. That, to the police, was a threat that demanded a response.

Space to Be Vulnerable

Death threats continued to abound, and my anxiety continued to escalate. One evening, before heading home from a public safety meeting following the protest, I met up with a couple of my friends, Matt and Bill. They're two white guys who always show up when I need them. Matt is a pacifist and Presbyterian pastor, and Bill is the former police officer and right-wing evangelical you met earlier in the book— someone who made a big shift in becoming.

As we talked about what was going on since the protest, with the death threats and online harassment, I broke down crying. Bill held me in his arms as I sobbed. Matt asked if he could spend the night on my doorstep. That way if the police or someone showed up to harm me or my family, he could put his body on the line and give us time to escape.

I thanked them both and told them I'd make it once I'd convinced myself I was okay—even though I definitely wasn't okay. What made it even more difficult was that many of my fellow Black movement organizers had taken steps away from me over that past week due to their own concern around what my new status meant for them. The anti-violence work depended on collaboration between the community and the police for success, and our protest concerned them. I heard a rumor that some were saying, "Ben stepped out there on his own; we can't put the work at risk. He's on his own." It was a hella lonely feeling.

When I did get home that evening, there was a police presence on my block. The police were frequently a presence in our neighborhood, but I'd never seen it like this. Several squad cars were lined up on the street. I thought to myself, *They hadn't shown this much of a heavy presence when the real crime was going down on my block, so why now?* That internal question was a rhetorical one, though. I knew the answer. They were on my block because it was me they were looking for. If they weren't authorized to haul me away in those silver cuffs, at least they could intimidate me.

I made my way past the cop cars and walked up my front steps and through my front door. When I got inside, I hid my anxiety from Gynelle. In my maladaptive way of experiencing trauma, I felt the way to protect my family was to hide my pain and project strength and courage. I had received what we call a love offering—a financial gift from my fellow preachers, many of whom were faith leaders who had been by my side in the throngs of the I-880 march. "How about we go to Santa Cruz," I suggested to her, "and get away for a week to chill out with the girls?" In reality, I was scared I could not protect them at home. And I was scared of what would happen *if* I couldn't protect them. Rather than offer Gynelle the truth, I made up a story about wanting to rest after a busy week.

Gynelle agreed to the trip. After she went to bed, I calmed myself down in a way that became too consistent over time as the work of occupying the radical middle became heavier and heavier: by drinking too much whiskey. Alcohol was becoming a coping mechanism, and I still didn't perceive the way it was creeping closer to a habit and a need.

This was all happening alongside another event: police showing up at an organization where I served on the board. Many people mistakenly thought I worked there because, if you googled me, that was the first organization to come up. Plainclothes police officers showed up there and claimed they had a meeting with me—which wasn't true. The same friend who showed up for me at the church where I preached was there that night, and he called me while they were still there. He sensed they were police officers, even though they weren't in uniform and didn't identify themselves as such.

I was out of town, so the young man asked me if I had a meeting scheduled. I told him no and told him to flat-out ask them if they were police officers. When he did, he said they stood silently and just stared at him. Then they gave him a police business card and left.

Later, I told this story to the Black officer I knew, and he confronted the officers and told them to knock it off. His confrontation with them occurred a couple of months after the harassment began, and it did finally stop.

Recalling this situation, and the fear I felt during that time for myself and my family, always makes me wonder: What happens to people who don't have the privilege and access that I had? People who can't call someone on the inside who has the power to stop such harassment? How many sisters and brothers experience this level of harassment (or worse) and have to suffer the trauma that comes from it, all without recourse? The work I do, the reason I continue, is in part for them.

That first night away with my family in Santa Cruz was truly a dark night of the soul. We had booked two adjoining rooms—one for ours girls and one for us. When we arrived at the hotel, I had so much going on inside of me, and yet I kept trying to project something totally different. I was anxious and wanted to break down and cry, but instead I told jokes and tried to make my wife and daughters smile and laugh. Meanwhile, I was hurting deep down.

After everyone went to bed, I just lay there on my side, silently, until I was sure Gynelle was asleep. Tears streaming down the side of my face, I finally got up and tiptoed to the chair in the living room of the suite. I kneeled down and cried quietly and prayed. I asked forgiveness of God because I was internalizing the trauma and felt I had done something wrong. I had put my family in danger, my fellow organizers weren't standing by me, and I had likely lost opportunities I had been working on for some time. I was also still grieving the fact that I had let down the young men years ago—the fellas who had first told me about the exploitative behaviors of the Oakland Police Department. Now I felt like it was all catching up to me.

I sat up most of the night, sleeping for only a couple of hours. I woke up and kept pretending I wasn't hurting. I did that because that's what I had trained myself to do since I was a kid whenever dealing with trauma. It was a survival mechanism, but it was also unhealthy.

Everything in me at that time just wanted to quit and disappear. Disappear from the threats on my life and the threats to my family. Disappear from the spotlight and microphones thrust in my face. Disappear from the fight of it all.

When you can't quantify the progress of your sacrifice, and particularly when you're from the Persecuted and Prevented quadrants, you internalize the perceived failure. White supremacy and patriarchy have immense cultural power—so much so that those victimized by them convince themselves that their inability to defeat them is their fault. It's sometimes called John Henryism: Black people working so hard to beat an unfair scenario and enduring such prolonged stress and discrimination that they experience chronic disease or health problems and die prematurely.

The overwhelm causes you to feel like you're always taking one step forward and two steps back. Dominant culture has a way of exhausting its victims into surrender and its leaders into internalizing that they weren't good enough to defeat something that should not exist in the first place.

Later, when I started therapy, my therapist would share with me an insight about the psychological terror of systemic racism on Black folks, an insight that helped me understand myself better. The only framework that Black men in the United States have for masculinity, historically speaking, is the one we've had since enslavement: white male masculinity. A lot of the framework of white male masculinity centers control and domination and a mentality that includes lording power over everyone. The Black man is getting his picture of masculinity from the white man, but he lives in a world where he will never *be* the white man. He lives in a world where the white man has always been able to come in, take his wife, take his children, and do whatever he wants with them. So the Black man has two choices: either fight the white man and die or allow his wife to be taken to the house to be abused and then try to comfort her upon her return. The psychological terror of that choice is immense. And what choice does a Black woman have? Fight back and die or submit to the abuse. Impossible choices all around.

We don't talk about these difficult parts of protest movements—the psychological terror, the historical roots of trauma, the self-destructive coping mechanisms—as often as we engage in hot rhetoric, hashtags, and media-rich moments. But they exist, and we must be aware they exist. They are journeys many of us travel alone—or at least feeling like we're alone. It can be very isolating, and we are left to contend with the thoughts and fears that try to overtake us.

While I didn't get some of the support I wanted from other Black leaders, my brother, Mike, was there for me, continuing to show that family (whether blood or chosen) is necessary if we're to do this work. We all need people who are there for who we are, not just what we can do. Activists from across the country who were tracking me were reaching out to me online with support, and that mattered. But the greatest support came from those close to me, those with whom I felt enough safety to share my fears and perceived failures.

If we don't have the privilege, means, or support to get away from the pressures for a short time, or for any time at all, we sit in that space or desperately try to trudge through it. There is no way this can *not* have an impact on us emotionally, psychologically, and physically. So get support, in whatever way you can. Find the people who will remind you that you are enough even when you can't pull down systems that have been in place for generations.

Put on Your Mask First

In the movement for radical belonging, the pressure is often turned up—*way* up. Whether that's because of the intensity of the moment or the intensity of threats you receive from the Powerful and the Privileged, who will go dangerously far to protect the status quo, it doesn't matter much. It's intense no matter what. And these threats or disparaging comments don't have to come from police or news media outlets or social media for them to be disturbing or frightening or harmful to your mental well-being. They may come from your local school board, members of your church, family and friends, or others in the community you previously considered allies.

Just as you hear flight crews instruct in case of emergency when you're on a plane: If there's a change in cabin pressure and oxygen masks drop from the panels above, put your masks on first before you help others. You've got to stay alive yourself if you're going to help others.

I had to have hard conversations within my nuclear family and with my parents. I had to get honest about where I had been dishonest while navigating this story of occupying the radical middle. I had to choose collective accountability over individual responsibility, and I had to learn to invite people to help me make healthy decisions about how engaged I would be in the activist work.

I had lots of guilt about this self-care initially because I only knew one way of participating: active leadership and all-in involvement. That way of participating made no room for personal healing and radical self-care as the bridge. I now believe we can have no belonging without healing, individually and collectively, being at the center.

One thing I wish I had done more of during that time is given myself even more time. I gave myself a week and then jumped back into the fight. I wanted a sabbatical but knew I couldn't afford it. Plus there was a combination of work addiction, love for the cause and the people, our need to be free, and the relationships I had through the work. All of this contributed. I needed a longer break, but I didn't take it. I wish I had because I hurt myself over the next couple of years by pushing myself beyond my capacity. The trauma of Trumpism during this season and the responsibility I felt to show up for our struggle were heavy burdens. Given all that we were all carrying, I deserved more grace toward myself than I was at that point able to give. This is one of my greatest learnings: putting on your oxygen mask only to rip it off too soon can be just as damaging as never having put it on at all.

This destructive pattern—taking care of myself for spurts of time but stopping too soon—continued for a few years, on and off. Getting stuck in it for a time taught me what happens when you engage in the work of radical belonging without the necessary work of radical self-care. Failure to center self-care ensures burnout, and we end up sacrificing our personal well-being and the well-being of those we care about most. Work addiction and alcohol abuse are how the pattern showed up for me, but I've seen it show up as many other destructive expressions for others. Sometimes the very thing that draws us into the work of making the world more just is the injury we have suffered because of the world's injustice. If we don't center radical self-care in our work for radical belonging, we end up becoming, at best, a commodity of the existing system or, at worst, a caricature of it. We've seen this before in social movements where leaders start off as colleagues, only to end up devouring each other privately and publicly. They end up weakening the very cause—widening the circle of human concern—they all care so deeply about.

Before I knew any better, I reemerged after the I-880 march and jumped back into the Movement for Black Lives just a week later. I was beginning to learn the power of intentional self-care, but I was still taking off my mask too soon. I continued leading statewide efforts to reduce violence and improve police and community relations. In this capacity, I led California in passing the strongest police transparency law in the country, SB 1421. This law would ensure that police officers who had records or provided unconstitutional policing would have their records tracked to ensure they couldn't just move to another police department after violating the public trust. We also helped to pass AB 953, also known as the Racial and Identity Profiling Act, which established the country's first statewide mandate for police officers to record who they were stopping so we could better understand how racial and identity profiling was happening. A very important part of this new law was establishing a statewide advisory board made up of community activists, law enforcement leaders, civil rights attorneys, and victims' rights advocates to bridge across difference and enforce the law. Vice President Kamala Harris, California attorney general at that time, nominated me to help lead this work. And we got AB 392, also called the California Act to Save Lives, passed as well. That law increases the restraints on police departments' use-of-force policies, which will reduce police killings.

All the while, we were hosting more than 120 trust-building events in fourteen different cities and fighting to stop then-President Trump's violence against immigrants. By 2018, I'd led thousands in marching in the streets to a detention center where migrant children were caged. We marched onto private property to face off with the law enforcement and private security holding them there. We were bringing attention to injustice, and much of our work was bearing fruit.

But there was always more work to be done, always more justice to be fought for. There was always more bridging desperately needed, always more radical belonging to work toward.

Don't Other Each Other

Some of the work that emerged for us to do involved bridging between Black and Jewish communities. The Movement for Black Lives was critical of the State of Israel's treatment of the Palestinians, calling Israel an apartheid state. That raised a lot of ire in the Jewish community. About the time I was experiencing threats and harassment, one of our sisters in the struggle, a Black woman active in the movement, got into hot water because she publicly gave support to Minister Louis Farrakhan. This led to even more frustration between the Black and Jewish communities. Jewish communities were calling on Black folks in the movement to denounce

Black Lives Matter and denounce Minister Farrakhan. But many of us refused to turn our backs on our sister. There would be no ganging up on Black people in public. We simply weren't going to get down with that. We weren't going to denounce our own struggle with Black Lives Matter and the voices within it.

No, we didn't all agree with everything that Minister Farrakhan said, and we even understood people who did not agree with *anything* he said. But at the same time, we were not going to be told what Black people should and should not denounce.

So there was a real feeling of consternation between the two communities. I started having conversations with some Jewish leaders, particularly those in faith-based community organizing who were also talking about the need for racial and economic justice. We facilitated conversations around bridging and figuring out what it could mean for us to come together across difference. What would happen if we had a conversation about Jewishness, Blackness, and Christianity?

Some of us decided to hold a two-day convention at the Synagogue in Bel Air, where we would learn how to listen to and hold one another's stories. At that event, I got a chance to understand more deeply why some of our Jewish relatives held the positions they did. I learned about pogroms, organized massacres of a particular ethnic group, and I learned in particular about the pogroms aimed to kill or expel Jewish people in Russia and Eastern Europe. I learned they'd been victims of genocide for over two thousand years. I learned about the Jewish custom of keeping five thousand dollars in cash in the top drawer of the bedroom dresser in case another ethnic cleansing were to start. With each new conversation, the rest of us became aware of the kind of sensitivities our Jewish brothers and sisters had, the type of discrimination they faced daily. The bridging felt palpable.

And I came to understand that many of them weren't aware of what it really means to be Black. We talked about the notion, for example, that I do not get to say whether I am Black or not, whereas religious and even ethnic identity is something many people can don or shed. They learned from us the ways in which structural injustice impacts Black people. Many came into that conference not understanding that for us, a Black woman getting attacked for expressing herself feels personal. When she gets attacked, it is not about a personality or an opinion. Seeing another Black person get verbally crucified, amid a historical legacy of lynching of Black people based on white discomfort, we weren't going to stand idly by and let it happen. We knew how inflammatory language could lead to actual violence, putting her child and her family in danger, and we just weren't having it.

Together, both sides began to more deeply grasp the ways both our communities had been impacted by ethnic cleansing and genocide. We came to understand that we were both highly protective of our cultures, which had—for both Black and Jewish people—been othered in dangerous ways. With this new knowledge and understanding, we began to facilitate new ways we could help Jewish folks more deeply understand the African American experience and vice versa. When we disagree, how do we choose to do something different, beyond calling on somebody to denounce somebody else or using power to force our way?

We left that conference with a measure of hope: that solutions to the immense social problems before us can be found by getting together, listening to each other, and understanding each other's experiences. Given the problems of today and of the future, getting together is not optional. It has never been optional. It is necessary.

Those of us who are marginalized and othered may have picked up some damaging practices of othering from our oppressors. We do what's been done to us. We utilize the tools that have been used against us. Sometimes we don't even realize it. That conference helped me learn that the best remedy for this is to pause, get close to the other person's pain, and try to step into the shoes of others across difference.

For the sickness that we are trying to combat is not racial in its origin. It definitely shows up in a racialized way because of how race has been codified into oppression and marginalization in this country for more than four hundred years. But the real sickness is an energy—an energy that, if we are not careful, we will allow to metastasize within our own marginalized groups. That energy commands that the only way for you to belong is for you to become me. It's narcissistic energy, rooted in colonialism, that suggests *our* way is the only way. It always leaves us with a zero-sum game of winners and losers.

I've experienced Black people doing it to each other. I've heard stories of women doing it to each other. I've heard stories of queer folks doing it to each other. Keep in mind that while we might be marginalized and be Persecuted or Prevented in one part of our life, we might be the Powerful and Privileged in another part. We need to think about how we deal with that energy. Because if we're not careful, it will consume us.

Instead, we have to commit to taking care of each other and ourselves. And in order for the movement for radical belonging to be sustainable, all of us engaged in this work have to learn how to practice gentleness, humility, empathy, and self-awareness. We need emotional intelligence to deal kindly with ourselves and others.

Some folks want to swear they woke up with a black glove on and rocking a four-inch Afro like the Black Panthers of the 1960s or that they have always been carrying a protest sign for the Movement for Black Lives in their hands. Truth is, though, none of us was born on the freedom train. We had to grow into that, each at our own pace. We each awaken at different times, triggered by different experiences. We can protest and organize ourselves all the way to burnout, if we're not careful. We have to be gentle and patient with ourselves first, and then we've got to be gentle and patient with others. We are all learning and becoming.

Recognize Your Breaking Point and Recalibrate

Even as I had begun to take self-care seriously, I realized my anger was being triggered frequently in those days. My anger and frustration with challenges *within* the movement—and with those individuals and organizations that worked to thwart our efforts or make us fearful—were eating away at me. I realized the anger was overtaking me when I began dehumanizing people who saw the world differently than me. I saw anger overtaking me when I began to entertain the notion that violence was a likely and perhaps viable strategy to get to belonging. My anger had moved from righteous to indiscriminate. It was becoming less informed by injustice itself—that's the righteous kind—and more informed by relieving angst, regardless of the impact on others.

But holding that anger within began to consume me. My heart condition was still worsening, I was still drinking too much, still sleeping too little, and still too addicted to the news. I stewed in the broth of everything that was wrong in the world and did not spend enough time in all that was hopeful.

The pressure had reached a critical level. I was at my breaking point. The only way to survive, to come out on the other side of the darkness, was to put comforting practices in place to feel safe in those vulnerable moments. I had to stop sticking out my chest and trying to just push through. Like I said earlier in the chapter, I had to put on my oxygen mask. And I had to learn how to leave it on rather than just taking a quick puff here and there and then running back into the fight.

I had to commit in a serious way to making changes *within* and not just changes around me. I am grateful for the many ways I have become since those days. But I still have to hold to those commitments and healthy boundaries like my life depends on it. Because it does.

Finding my way back to the work, as I'm engaging in now, has been a journey of healing. Everyone's oxygen mask will look different, but mine looked like getting in therapy and getting a life coach. It meant embracing mental health support from a medical professional that included medication and weight loss. It meant getting support with reversing my increasing dependency on alcohol. It would eventually look like quitting my job, taking a ninety-day sabbatical, and living alone for a month to reconnect to myself.

Here are some of the self-care practices I put in place:

Slow down. In my personal life, I had to develop tools that will help me slow down. I was often caught up in the swirl—whether that swirl was occurring around me or within me. As a result, my mind was often racing, which can create fertile ground for anxiety to creep in and take root.

One tool I use is what I call "speed bumps" to slow myself down. For example, I play vinyl records on a record player and listen to them while relaxing in my office. This allows me to not only slow down and enjoy some good music that often takes me back to happier times, it also allows me to set my phone to the side—or, better yet, to turn it off. Stepping away from all the screens and shutting out the noise that comes through our devices is good for your peace of mind. Your speed bump could be anything you enjoy doing that helps you consciously slow down. Maybe it's yoga or breathwork. Maybe it's a hobby like cooking, gardening, or getting out in nature for some fresh air. Or maybe it's quality time with loved ones.

Disrupt the dominant voice. I also learned to disrupt the dominant voice. My friend, author Brian K. Woodson, talks about the power of the enslaver's whip in the mind of the enslaved. Slaveholders would whip the enslaved, and the pain of that would cause them to work harder. Then they would just crack the whip in the air, and just the memory of the whipping was enough to speed up the work. Eventually, the enslaver wouldn't have to even be present, and the whip didn't have to be visible because that whip would now have taken up residence in the enslaved person's own mind. The nature of the trauma itself would demand harder work.

Getting the dominant voice out of my head has involved challenging false beliefs about work, about not taking care of myself, about what I must do in order to receive love and respect, about what is required of me to be safe. That is the whip that often cracks loudly in my mind. Exorcising the demon of white supremacy out of my own heart is the work.

In practice, this looks like asking myself a lot of questions. It means when I plan out my time, I ask myself, "Do I really need to do all of this?" and "Why?" It means asking, "Do I really need to be at these meetings?" and "Do I really believe this is the right approach?" This practice has also meant I invest in a coach who will ask these questions of me when I'm not willing to ask them of myself.

Push toward reflection. Reflection is an important part of self-awareness and becoming. I install breaks in my calendar for the purpose of reflection. I block out parts of my annual calendar to "get off the plantation" and ask myself, "Why am I picking cotton?" I also have a practice of creating a monthly time budget, which helps me understand how much external time I'm spending taking care of others versus taking care of myself. When my percentage of taking care of others is too high, I work on making decisions differently so that I can shift some of that time to taking care of myself.

When I realize a trend I don't like, I engage with more therapy and work on continuing the healing journey. I've learned, and am learning, that reflection is my salvation, not another protest.

Be intentional about your connections. As I mentioned, sometimes this work can be isolating. So I am now very intentional about my connections and making sure people around me keep me grounded and balanced. These are individuals who help me remember my why, as well as why it's critical for me to take care of myself.

In addition to family, friends, and those who love you, make sure you have an open line to ten people who are part of your community. Your family and friends watch out for you, but you need to have others you are watching out for. I have folks who are there to watch out for me, and I have folks I watch out for too. I also make an effort to stay proximate to the Persecuted and Prevented in a way that's sustainable, keeping in mind that it's easy for the pendulum to swing too far to one side or the other. I believe the power is, again, in the radical middle.

Allow yourself to grieve. Pushing through won't do. You have to create space for your feelings, for your pain. Grief can be brought on by something you experienced personally or something you witnessed in the news or in your community. Either way, it affects you, and sometimes you may have to step back, take a break, and allow yourself to process what you're feeling. Ignoring your pain does not mean that it's not there or that it will simply go away over time. Also remember we each grieve differently and need whatever amount of time that process requires.

Make time for joy. In the same way that it is healthy to make room for your grief, it's imperative you make time and space for joy. Laughter is healthy, and moments of levity are healing. People often marvel at the ability of Black folks to embrace joy in spite of the pain and oppression that have been our experience for generations. This isn't to say we ignore the pain or are immune to it. That, indeed, is another false narrative about Black folks, one that makes us more susceptible to violence and mistreatment from others who are under the illusion that we don't feel as any human feels. Trust me, the pain is there. But the joy is there as well. And embracing that joy is an act of resistance—and radical self-care—in and of itself.

Rest. Whether it's getting your speed bumps in place or simply shutting down your phone and getting a good night's sleep, incorporate rest into your activism. The only way to keep going is knowing when you need to stop for a while.

Rest, too, is an act of resistance. Nap Ministry founder Tricia Hersey writes about what she calls "grind culture," a blend of white supremacy and capitalism, in her book *Rest Is Resistance: A Manifesto*. "Resting as a form of resistance will be part of a lifelong unraveling. A mind shift, a slow and consistent practice filled with grace," Hersey writes. "We must imagine a new way, and rest is the foundation for this invention. We should use every tool we have to constantly repair what grind culture has done to us. We will be disrupting and pushing back against grind culture for a lifetime."

We also need to resist the idea that we're supposed to solve a four-hundred-year problem within our lifetime—without rest, nonetheless. To even attempt to do so is exhausting. We are trying to change a world that has been functioning in a certain way for centuries. And the present world is not exactly rolling out welcome mats for change. So, with imagination, we have to look into a future world that we may not get to live within. As my friend Terry Supahan helped me learn to ask, "What are the things we have to do today in order to fuel the world that people will live in seven generations from now?" That perspective might actually help us rest a bit more. We're playing the long game here.

To get there, we each have to contribute where we can and remember to take care of ourselves. As the prophet Nehemiah said in the Jewish scriptures, "Build a wall where your house exists." In other words, ask yourself: How can I help solve the problem that's in front of me? How can I do my part without being consumed by the work? Asking these questions can prevent you from being destroyed by the calamity around you.

Show yourself some grace. You will question yourself. You will ask yourself, "Is this really worth it?" The work I am most proud of is the bridging work we did in Oakland, and let's face it: that work had massive ups and downs, major wins, and huge failures. So know that yes, it is worth it. And so is the risk. When I was at the frontline of the protest march, as a man in a clerical collar, I knew there was strength in what my faith represented. I risked being in front for those fighting just as hard behind me. Sometimes I dodged batteries, bricks, and bottles of urine hurled at the police because I was positioned between protesters and police.

Still, there are times when I don't want to risk, particularly when I am experiencing comfort or a perceived sense of safety. Who wants to risk that? Nobody. But we must. Even in my spiritual practice, as a person trying to follow Jesus, I wonder, "How can I follow Jesus without spilling my caramel macchiato with foam on the top?" I'd love to figure out how to live the right way while maintaining the most power and agency and safety and comfort that I possibly can. That's just the truth! But moving toward belonging is about risking the notions of how we've made meaning, and it's about changing what it means to be safe, and it's about choosing to take chances. Allow yourself grace as you find, lose, and reestablish your footing here.

Be gentle. Whether you're new to this work or you've been part of the movement for years, remember that you are going to make mistakes. You are not perfect; none of us is. Be gentle. Remain grounded in and committed to your intention of contributing to the creation of a world where we all practice radical belonging. Choose to learn the lessons, grow through it, and then do something about it.

8

Do Something Now

My dad grew up in the South, a child amid Jim Crow racism and terrorism against Black folks. When he was thirteen, he met Dr. Martin Luther King Jr. Dr. King had come to his junior high school in Goldsboro, North Carolina, to train students about nonviolence so they could participate in student lunch-counter demonstrations, protests, and sit-ins.

As a junior high school student, my dad and a bunch of other boys had a simple yet profound experience with Dr. King when he took them to look at the backside of the water fountains. At the time, water fountains were labeled "whites only" and "colored only." He showed them that the pipes running to the "white" water fountains were the same pipes that were running to the "colored" water fountains. My dad said it was the first time he realized they were drinking the same water as their white counterparts. He hadn't known they weren't drinking a substandard version of water, that they were literally drinking the same water.

After this mind-opening experience, he participated in a protest with Dr. King along with others, and they were arrested. He and the other young people were put in a paddy wagon, taken to jail, and shoved shoulder to shoulder in a cell. My father said the children were urinating and defecating on themselves because of the extreme fear, and the white police officers stood outside the jail cell laughing at them all. An image and a trauma he will never forget.

Then when my dad was twenty-two years old, he was drafted into the Vietnam War and was in Vietnam from 1969 to 1971. But before that, Dad told me that he spent time draft-dodging, a practice known by many who resisted the draft in Vietnam. He was trying to avoid the violence that the system was demanding he participate in, and he avoided it for as long as he could.

My dad recounted this part of his life to me over breakfast at IHOP one morning. The draft required young men to enlist in the military and head to the war. My dad first received this call in Detroit, Michigan, where he was working in an auto plant. He was flagged down before his lunch by another Black man, who was the manager. "Mac," his manager said, "we just received a telegram from Uncle Sam asking if you work here." This was a known signal that he was going to be drafted. So Dad told his manager to send his check to his mother and left for lunch, never to return. He went to Kansas City, Missouri, and changed his vocation from the auto industry to the airline industry. He enrolled in the United Airlines training program, which was heavily recruiting Black workers at the time after the passage of the Civil Rights Act. He remained there awhile until he got word again, from another Black colleague, that the government was snooping around for draft-dodgers. He left Kansas City and went to Albuquerque, New Mexico, where he took a job at a school cafeteria while also being a home aide for an elderly woman who provided a room for him on her property. It wasn't too long before the government came looking for him there.

Dad then left Albuquerque and headed for San Francisco—my birth city and the place he would meet my mother. He attended City College and lodged at the local YMCA, where young men could rent rooms by the week and stay under the radar. It was there that the government finally caught up with him. While he initially refused to go to Vietnam, he was told that if he didn't comply, his younger brothers would be drafted and sent to the war.

In essence, saving his own life meant endangering his younger siblings' lives. So finally, at that intersection, he agreed to submit himself to the draft. At the time, a family would not suffer the hardship of more than one son getting drafted. So my dad spared his brothers and went.

To prepare him to become a soldier, the US government took him and his fellow recruits into the bayou of Louisiana. There they trained them on how battles would be in the jungles of Vietnam. They kept showing them pictures of Vietnamese soldiers on wooden pop-ups and trained them to repeatedly shoot them. It was a way to dehumanize and other the Vietnamese in the minds of the young soldiers. Then one day, my dad said, "They woke us up, and forty-eight hours later, I was jumping off an airplane into the rice paddies of Vietnam and dropped into the middle of a war zone."

As he saw it, the US government that was once persecuting him was now calling on him to persecute others in their own country. Soon after he arrived in Vietnam, he was sent to burn down Vietnamese villages and shoot all who were deemed the enemy. For my dad and many others, this was the cost of staying alive, the cost of coming home. The government had put them in a situation where, if they wanted to survive, they had to behave in a way that was against their morals and values. Researchers call this *moral injury*: when human beings are thrust into situations in which obeying orders violates their own moral code and conscience.

On one mission, Dad, who was a sergeant, led his company of soldiers into a particular village. An elderly Vietnamese woman came running out of the village waving to him and yelling, "GI, GI, GI!"

"For some reason, I stopped," he remembered, shaking his head a bit over our breakfast as he recalled the scene. "We didn't shoot her; we didn't harm her." Instead, he leaned down to hear what she had to say.

"She got close to my ear and whispered, 'Martin Luther King know you here?'"

At that moment, all his experience of living in the South and being a victim of racial violence throughout his life came flooding back to him. In this faraway land, he stood there as a Black man and reconnected with himself. Those words were all he needed to remind himself that although he was an agent of the United States in this war in Vietnam, he was still a human being. He was not meant to be an agent of the violence he experienced back home.

"I did not want to do that," Dad told me. "I did not want to be a part of that."

Everything changed in that moment. Instead of ordering his soldiers to burn the village, he went to the watchtower of that village and bribed the soldier stationed there with a bottle of Johnnie Walker Red whiskey. "Listen. We're not going to burn this village up," my dad told him. "We give you this Johnnie Walker Red; you just let us pass through."

For the rest of his time in Vietnam, Dad bribed his way out of burning down any villages. He traded Johnnie Walker Red and marijuana for the chance to not participate in that work. His actions not only safeguarded the Vietnamese people; my dad, as the sergeant and leader of his platoon, brought all his troops back alive and well.

My dad decided, in that moment, to become someone different. He became a different version of himself—and he kept becoming. It wasn't that he even really tried to become something or do something different. It was that a Vietnamese elder helped him access a piece of his humanity that he did not know was there. And his choice to become meant real change for the people he was leading.

This is a reminder that who we need to be is already within us. It's there. Have the courage to become it. And then do something with it.

Keep Becoming

I am working to become a better version of myself. I am working to evolve as a leader, and I am working to end gun violence. My journey to become is ongoing and continual and has heightened from the first day I saw Blaine sunbathing in the middle of the street. It is strengthened by stories like my dad's.

I am also fighting to create a world where we all belong. For centuries, we have been told stories that some people in this world are less human than others. These inherited stories are false and damaging, but they perpetuate the myths that we should exclude some people, take away their voices and opportunities, and deny them belonging so that we can stay safe. We've been conditioned to accept these stories, and we have chosen to adopt them as principles that form our beliefs.

But we have another choice. We can choose to believe we are radically interconnected, that we are deeply connected across difference, because we have the power within us to do so. But we must start by redirecting our inclination toward self-interest to the notion of a collective interest of all. And we must do the work necessary to achieve this goal.

Understand the Assignment

We must figure out which values we share, which hopes we share, what pain we share, and, yes, which differences we have. But now let's say you do all that. Let's say you still find yourself unsure if you belong. What if you're like my brother, Michael, that first day he arrived in Ferguson? As a Black man and a man of faith, he assumed he belonged; he went there and used his body in protest. But some people still treated him like an outsider, and he wasn't sure he belonged there. Or what if you're a white guy like my friend Bill, who was also in Ferguson with us but who wasn't so sure he should cross the street to join me? In those circumstances and ones like it, what do you do if you're not sure if you belong or not?

But hear me on this: If you are willing to hold one another's perspective, you belong. If your spirit is telling you to bridge, you belong. In other words, if you are asking yourself if you belong, simply tell yourself yes. I believe we hesitate to embrace our own belonging—and to make others feel as though they belong—because we are merely looking at how and when we can find the courage to take that first risky step into someone's story. I did it by taking that first meeting with Bill, who was very different from me, back in 2012. Bill did it by crossing the street to join protesters who were very different from him.

Maybe there's something burning inside you—something that has been ignited due to an experienced injustice. Your spirit understands the assignment. Or maybe you're where Bill was—deconstructing what you believe, not sure what to think, but feeling called to do something. Maybe you're where I was, and your intellect is telling you to listen to someone like Jabari—someone who has come calling, someone who is calling you to be someone better than you are or even better than you thought you needed to be. Or maybe you want to live in a way that's driven by love versus one that's driven by fear.

If you're itching, aching, hungry enough, hurt enough, pissed off enough, or irate enough to get to the table, bridging is the activity to help you begin to make change. When you have the capacity, it becomes an opportunity for you to discover new outcomes that would otherwise not be available.

Remember this too: Not every dynamic where we have stress, injustice, or anxiety is an opportunity to bridge. Bridging is not a panacea. Bridging doesn't solve every conflict. It is simply the first step in understanding each other and making room at the table for each other's stories.

March On

When I returned to Ferguson in October 2014, it was Columbus Day weekend. But for all of us in the fight for justice, it was the Weekend of Resistance. After the violence of Bloody Sunday against unarmed Black people, Dr. Martin Luther King Jr. had made a national call from Selma, Alabama, that people of values and goodwill would come to Selma and join a march across a bridge. Similarly, young activists from Ferguson were making a call for a weekend of nonviolent action: to raise awareness around the demand to arrest Darren Wilson, the Ferguson police officer who had killed Mike Brown two months earlier. Several protests were planned under the banner of "Ferguson October," and I, along with other Christian, Muslim, and Jewish clergy, planned to participate. My friend Bill, eager to join the bridging, came along.

We wanted the Ferguson Police Department to understand the gravity of this moment for Michael Brown's family, the community, and the national consciousness. We wanted a meeting with the police chief, to bring him to the table and create space for a change of direction that would hold Officer Darren Wilson accountable for murdering our dear young brother just a few months earlier. We were ready to fill the jails with us—the preachers and imams and rabbis and other adults—instead of our young people.

The energy of protesting and various forms of demonstrating had not waned in Ferguson; the community had been out faithfully every night for the past sixty days, ever since Mike Brown was murdered. Tensions were running high, and the city was a powder keg waiting to explode. Police were taking an extremely aggressive posture toward the public protests, which are constitutionally protected.

When we arrived on the scene, we did a healing ritual, in which a Black pastor lay on the ground to bring forth the Black ancestors who had died due to police violence. We began reciting their names. As we did, Bill—representing all that he was as a white former cop and evangelical pastor—knelt down and chalked an outline around the pastor's body. Each name of a fallen one received an outline, and each name received a candle placed along the chalk line around the body. Name after name after name. As each name was read, I felt a pain well up from deep within me, one I didn't know I had. It erupted into tears that I could not control.

And then came the rain: lightly at first and then in sheets. People started shielding the burning candles with their umbrellas; it was like we felt the need to shield the lives of these people we were remembering, even after those lives had been extinguished. Somehow the flickering flames of those candles, in that moment, signified everything.

I was offered an umbrella, but I refused it. The soaking sheets of rain washed over me, and I lifted my face to it, to catch every drop of it. I felt baptized by this water from the sky, this pouring out of water that came over me in this moment of anguish.

I stood alongside hundreds, and together we wept: for Michael Brown, for all those unarmed Black people who had been killed by police, for the travesty that was our condition as Black people in this country. Seeing Bill weeping with me, and seeing other white people who sympathized, helped me recognize in that moment that we shared this burden. We linked arm in arm, and we walked.

We were nearly four hundred people. Together I marched along with my peers, including Dr. Cornel West, Rev. Osagyefo Sekou, my brother, Pastor Renita Lamkin, Dr. Traci Blackmon, Rev. Jim Wallis, Rev. Alvin Herring, and Dr. Iva Carruthers. The crisp fall air was filled with emotional cries for due process. With words as our weapons, along with our sheer presence, we amassed. The rain continued to pour, and we continued to our destination, which was the police station.

The police department met us there with their weapons. They set up a protest line with law enforcement standing next to each other as sort of a human barricade, but behind them were officers armed with riot gear, helmets, and wooden nightsticks. Not unlike the tools used against civil rights demonstrators.

My brother was in the row in front of me, his arms linked with Dr. Cornel West's. They marched until they could move no more. The police grabbed my brother and dragged him to the ground. I watched them carry him off to be arrested. As they carried Mike out of my sight toward the back of a police station, I knew that if he was willing to put his body on the line for this cause, there was no way I was not going to do the same.

I approached the police line with other leaders. With their strength and courage by my side, we began to sing that old Negro spiritual "Wade in the Water."

Wade in the water,
Wade in the water, children.
Wade in the water,
God's going to trouble the water.

We began to sing; an energy rose out of me and those with whom I stood. On both sides of me were two white ministers: one man, one woman. Strangers by name but kindred in spirit. There we stood, arm in arm, singing this Negro spiritual with all our strength, asking God to trouble the water. We would continue to wade in the water as long as we could. And here, on the streets in the pouring rain, we were ready to trouble the water too.

Every bit of everything was coursing through my veins, and then I moved. I stepped up to the police line. With inches between us, I demanded that the police repent of their evil deeds and said that I stood there as a man of the cloth to receive their confession. I was nose to nose with white police officers with their riot gear and face guards. I moved, pushing forward with my body, every bit of everything speaking to me to do so.

One of the command staff locked eyes with me from behind the riot line. He shouted, "If you don't move, we will arrest you!"

I didn't move.

I felt hands upon my body as they pulled me through their line and took my body down to where I landed on my knees on the wet ground. Handcuffs cinched my wrists. I was arrested and led to a processing desk set up outside the police station. There I joined about twenty other protesters who were getting arrested. I immediately saw my brother,

Michael, standing there in handcuffs. We smiled at each other. We may have been in a bad situation, but at least we were in it together.

A Black police officer held my cuffs. He was in his early forties, about five-foot-nine with a muscular build. He had strong eyes and a clean-shaven face. Officially, in his brown St. Louis County Sheriff's uniform, he asked me where I was from and why I was there. I told him that I was from the Bay Area in California. A moment of awkward silence fell between us.

Then I looked at him, and I began to share my story about the only time I'd stared down a gun. I told him about how the police had racially profiled me and detained me because they said I "fit the description" of someone who had committed an armed robbery in the neighborhood.

The police officer said, "Well, what if you *were* that individual they were looking for, and they hadn't stopped you? What if you were the guy they were looking for, and you had the gun, and they didn't roll up on you or jump out with guns drawn? They themselves would have risked injury."

I said, "But I was not the guy."

His voice hardened. "But what if you *were* the guy?"

I stared at him and said quietly and tersely, "But I was *not* the guy."

He got quiet. After a moment, he said, "I know what you're saying. But I'm just saying we have to make sure we go home safe at night."

"And I just want to ensure that I go home safe at night," I responded. "And here's the thing, Officer. Y'all are trained police officers. I am not a trained citizen. I'm just a citizen.

I don't go through six months to figure out how to be a citizen; I'm just a citizen."

He acquiesced a bit. "Well, I'm hearing what you're saying," he said. "But as police officers, we just want to figure out how to go home at night. And I know you're trying to figure out how to go home at night." He paused. "So I don't know. Then that just means we're gonna have to figure out how to get something different."

With about as much control as I could manage, I said, "Well, Officer, that's the very reason I came to Ferguson, Missouri: because we need to get something different."

So there we stood in the back of the Ferguson police station, me in handcuffs and him standing there holding my arm as my arresting officer. And we continued talking. We had a conversation in which we began to bridge.

I don't know what it feels like to walk in that police officer's shoes, to take on the risks that he does daily. I don't know what it feels like to have to kiss your family, thinking that it might be the last time you ever see them again. I don't know what it feels like to have to make a split-second decision, knowing your reaction could cause someone to die. And even though he's a Black man, he didn't know entirely what it feels like to be me either. He didn't know the threats and harassment I'd received.

That police officer and I both recognized that the status quo wasn't sufficient. We needed to create a story where we both belonged, where we both could go home at the end of the day. But right now, we had only the existing story within the police force, which says they have to other a person in order to get that. With Mike Brown, the othering became deadly.

After being arrested and jailed by the officer, I sat in the jail with many of the other leaders who had traveled to Ferguson to stand in solidarity with the young people. Renowned academic and public intellectual Dr. Cornel West was among group, and I watched as he was also being processed. This includes having a sheriff hold you by the arm and move your physical body around from place to place. It involves being told to take your shoes off, remove your shoestrings, remove your tie. It is a very dehumanizing experience.

While this was happening, Dr. West, to my surprise, kept saying, "Thank you, good brother. Thank you, good sister," to the officers. The police would move him from one stage of the booking process to the next stage, and he would again say, "Thank you, good brother," or "Thank you, good sister."

At a certain point, my brother, Mike, asked him the question that was on all of our minds. "Doc, how can you keep calling these people 'good brother' and 'good sister'?" It was a fair question considering that the officers booking us and putting us in jail had not shown us, that day or in the many days before, any respect in our pursuit of justice. It was a fair question given the story of exclusion and other-ing and violence that we all found ourselves living in.

"Oh, good brother, good brother, good brother," Dr. West told Mike, a smile on his lips. "Always leave the light on—because you never know when they'll come home!"

What a profound statement for what it means to be a prisoner of hope and to work for a world of radical belonging. Radical belonging means that even when faced with people who are working to constrict the circle of human concern instead of widen it, we can see people as our siblings. We can leave the light on.

Heed the Call

If you are someone who has some proximity to the levers of change around the status quo, I want to compel you—above all others—to do something. I challenge you to be more human. I shouldn't have to—it's a choice you should make on your own. We can all be guilty of becoming intoxicated by power and privilege. With this knowledge, and even with this privilege and power, we still have to choose to become more human. We have to choose love.

"Power without love is reckless and abusive, and love without power is sentimental and anemic," Dr. King said. "Power at its best is love implementing the demands of justice, and justice at its best is power correcting everything that stands against love." This prophetic quote reminds us that belonging must exist in cultural and structural environments where love is the culture of belonging and power is the structure. Oftentimes, those who want power want power without love, and those who want love want love without power. Dr. King encourages us to accept that you actually can't have one without the other; there is a balance that happens, and the atmosphere of belonging we should strive for happens when folks have agency to cocreate with love and power together.

We also have to remember to listen to the othered to understand what their needs truly are. Belonging will always be communicated to us best by those who are most subordinated or marginalized—by those who are closest to the pain. In other words, the people closest to the problem in any given scenario are closest to the solutions. Our journey to becoming a new version of ourselves is about lifting up those voices and supporting and following the leadership of those most impacted by the pain—oppression, discrimination, hatred. They are the ones who will help us get to belonging. They are the ones who understand what it is like to have less power, to have less protection, to be closest to the agony of our societies.

Women will help us undo patriarchy.

LGBTQ+ relatives will help us undo homophobia.

Immigrants will help us undo xenophobia.

Black people will help us undo racism.

And yet all too often, those with the most power are threatened by the idea of widening their circle of belonging because they equate it with giving up power, and that idea is terrifying to them. What they need to be understood is they're not just giving something up; they're also gaining something back: love from the rest of society, a deeper sense of interconnectedness, and a fuller expression of their humanity.

As human beings, we tend to operate from a scarcity mindset rather than one of abundance. Power is seen as a sacred commodity because there is so little of it to go around. We've been trained to strive for power—and if we get some, to not let go of it. And so many of us hold on to whatever power we have as a way to feel safe.

We must unlearn this behavior, and we must encourage those who have the most power to both leverage some of it to help others and to authentically share it in a way that creates both equality and social equity.

Let us figure out how to be aware of the differences between us—the differences in our cultures, religions, political views, and life experiences—in ways that really help us support one another. Instead of managing difference through segregating ourselves, by othering each other, or by saming, we can manage difference through curiosity.

Belonging is about building a bigger space that has the reality—the truth—of both our worlds. It requires new practices, new language, new behaviors, and new ways of being human together that we did not have in our separate spaces.

We can do this.

Do Something

In the movement of radical belonging, we each have to commit to doing something. What that something looks like will be different for each of us. But the commitment itself is essential.

If you are a white person, you are going to think about what it means for you to help create more belonging as it relates to Black people, Indigenous folks, and people of color. If you are a man, you are going to have a conversation about gender and creating more belonging for all who identify as women. If you are a Christian, you're going to be thinking about what it means to create belonging for Jewish, Muslim, and nonreligious folks, who experience a kind of othering that we need to be aware of and address.

Now in all these cases, keep in mind that although you didn't personally create the system that benefits you, you did inherit it, and you likely reap rewards from its existence.

There are a lot of ways I don't feel safe in this world. Being Black in America will do that to you. But when it comes to my Christianity in America, I'm in the Powerful and Privileged space. I'm a dude, so that means I'm in that dominant space as it relates to gender. I'm able-bodied, so I'm advantaged. Class-wise, I have enough coins to do some things that I enjoy doing. That's a privilege.

None of us is one thing. Many of us are advantaged by society in some ways and disadvantaged by others, but some people are much more marginalized than others. Let us hold that and do something to rectify it so that equity exists for us all.

Many Faces of Belonging

There is no one way to practice belonging, just as there is no one world where everyone belongs (at least not yet). Belonging work can be sitting with people to change the way an organization functions or how a family makes decisions. Belonging is also protesting on the streets to challenge public systems affecting those who are most disadvantaged. What belonging always entails is challenging the systems that oppress some and advantage others.

The world is infected, at every level, with othering. Othering happens in individual and interpersonal expressions and in structural and cultural ways, making it present in every aspect of our lives. This means we can't attack it with a policy here or a reform there. We can't "burn it all down and start over" because we'd have to burn ourselves down in the process. Othering impulses live within all of us, to some degree. As we say in community organizing, we have to take the work as a loaf of bread and cut it into slices.

We have to all work on the project together, engaging it from the places and positions we find ourselves. Everybody doesn't have to do the same thing, but everybody has to do something!

I did a training at one of the big tech companies in 2019, and we were working with employees of color. A Black woman came up to me after the presentation and confided in me about how much she was struggling with othering at work. She had left her job at *Essence,* a Black-owned company, and had to take a job at this tech company, which has been called the most powerful company in the world. Her new role here was, in her words, a "dream job" in terms of salary, stock options, and other perks of a high-powered tech position. She shared, "Brother, I just got to tell you, the level of violence that I feel in my body being in a room with seven out of ten white men and them gaslighting me, questioning the skills I have." She said, "I have been a brilliant presenter, but I'm fumbling over my words. I can't find my power, my magic. I'm about this close to just going back to *Essence* because I'd rather have the safety of just being able to be me. But then my heart hurts because this job, financially, could change the trajectory of my family for a generation."

She paused. "I feel like I'm having to make a choice," she said. "Do I take care of myself? My mental health? My emotional health? Or do I take care of my family? It's such an unfair position."

Unfortunately, her experience is far from unique; so many Black women experience similar acts of othering at work each day. "I'm thirty-four years old, and I've done everything right," she told me. "All I'm asking is, can I be in this space? This company brought me here because of my brilliance. And then when you bring me here, you create this environment where I'm set up for failure."

Her story, and that of so many others, is what pushed me to go beyond activism around community violence and police violence and start engaging in corporate spaces. We need to figure out how to implement belonging into organizational structures. Othering is like a disease that shows up differently in different bodies—countries, governments, nonprofits, families, and corporations—in different ways. So the manifestation of belonging will need to look different, depending on the context.

Bridging never ends. Difference always exists, and our practice of belonging will require us to keep this skill sharp and in use. Let's go back to the Quadrants for a moment: the Powerful, Privileged, Persecuted, and Prevented. Belonging requires us to break down the barriers between us and to undo the structures, systems, and practices that divide us. To accomplish this, we must move from the back corners of our sectarian and segmented identities within the quadrant and move toward the middle. When we've moved closer to each other, we can begin to build shared humanity by bridging: experiencing each other across difference. We can't break down the entire quadrant at one time, but we can begin with one step, and then another, and then another, until we've reached our goal. The key is to stay in it for the long haul, even if it looks different for you than when you started.

Adjust but Don't Tap Out

As I mentioned earlier, Frederick Douglass wrote, "Power concedes nothing without a demand." And that's true. But demand doesn't always look the same. Demand doesn't have to be loud. In fact, the loudest voices in a movement or a family or a country are often not the voices closest to the pain. Sometimes they're the ones with the most to lose from this disruption of the status quo. Demand can look like protesting with a sign in your hand and a fist up in the air. Demand can also look like a united front from employees who insist on policy changes within an organization that will guarantee more diversity, equity, and opportunities for all. Ask yourself: What does my demand need to look like for the power that I'm trying to engage?

In my family structure, for example, my kids have less power and privilege than my wife and I do in our nuclear family. If they want to get more agency in our family, I can tell you right now: Protesting or boycotting or making demands is not going to work. That's not the right tactic for trying to create change in our home. But starting a dialogue, asking for a conversation, making your case with logic and love? That might just work. How you make your demand matters, and our established relationship will help advance the results. The demand that may work in one setting will need to be adjusted in different settings to reach the goal.

So be willing to adjust how you make demands on a system. Find the style of change-making and the type of radical belonging work that fit your personality and your life. And do the radical self-care thing we talked about in chapter 7. But please, whatever you do, don't tap out.

Black folks don't have the privilege of tapping out. We *have* to stay engaged because, often, our lives depend on it. One of the reasons we stay proximate to all this radical belonging stuff is because our own survival is at stake. We don't get to say, "I'm not focusing on that right now." Or even if you do choose that posture, and even if you think you have somehow "risen above" othering, it can still find you—even in your own homes.

Harvard professor Henry Louis "Skip" Gates was arrested in 2009 by police officers responding to a call that a man was breaking into a home. Even though he was entering his own home in his own bourgeois neighborhood near the prestigious university where he taught, and even though he is a lauded professor and public figure, it didn't matter. In a more tragic example, Breonna Taylor and her boyfriend experienced othering in her own home in 2020. As a result, an unarmed, innocent woman was killed by police and is no longer with us. Botham Jean, Atatiana Jefferson, and others have been killed by police officers inside their own homes. If a white person or police officer sees you and says you don't belong here—even when the "here" is your own home—they literally can leverage the power of the US government against your Black body.

This is what othering does. It sets up and oppresses people and offers no choices for them to move forward. That's why my call is to compel the Powerful and Privileged to do something. You must make some different decisions—because everybody else's survival depends on it.

Step into Your Power

As you commit to this journey of creating a world of radical belonging, I challenge you again with that question that is bigger than "What will you do?" I ask you instead: Who will you *become*?

Look to what keeps you up at night. Of the stories that come to the newsfeed on your phone or the headlines on the radio, what are the most disturbing or seem the most accessible? Begin there. And if you're worried about if you're ready or not, don't sweat it. You picked up this book; I believe you are ready.

Wherever you find yourself is where you can begin to build, where you can begin to bridge, where you can begin to make change. You may look within the quadrants of the Powerful, Privileged, Persecuted, and Prevented, and as you begin to bridge with others, you may begin to think about how to undo the structures, systems, or practices that work to divide folks rather than keep them together. You may look at the pain and insert yourself close to it. You might pick up a bullhorn or a laptop and get to work.

You don't have to have anything to get started, really: just a will, which I believe is already within you, and a way. Do the work your way, with the intention of expanding the circle of human concern and creating radical belonging for others. We see this from our foremothers, fathers, sisters, and brothers. Dr. King's methods toward freedom were different from those of Oskar Schindler, yet both fought for the right to live. Yuri Kochiyama's approach to social justice was different from Gloria Steinem's, yet both fought for equality. Your approach might be different from mine, yet we both want peace. The fight is always there; how you join the battle is up to you. But join you must.

So if you're feeling anxiety around race, or if you're feeling anxiety around what's going on at work with your team, or if you're feeling anxiety about how your dad voted, get in there. Get to work. Build. Bridge. Belong. This call for belonging is not about saving ourselves as individuals in terms of the resources that we have or the access we have been granted. Belonging is about saving our very humanity.

If you are not thriving, then I am not thriving; if you do not have peace, then I do not have peace; if you do not belong, then I myself do not belong. There is an Nguni expression, *ubuntu*, which means "humanity" and "I am because we are." It is part of a larger phrase, *Ubuntu ngumtu ngabanye abantu*: "A person is a person through other people." The Mayans use a term *in lak'ech*, which means "You are the other me." When we truly see one another, we literally *become*. The challenges to belong cannot be resolved in isolation but can only be resolved when we are existing together across differences.

We have to be willing to meet each other on the porch in peace, to make room for each other, to listen to each other. Even if, at first, we might be inclined to presume the other person or group doesn't belong. Or if we have fears or doubts about our own belonging. Do not hide in the back corners of your quadrant. Welcome your neighbor. Have a conversation. Listen not with a need to agree or disagree but with an open heart and a desire to try to understand their perspective. Pause, just as I did with the brother sitting on my porch—the porch that was once his—in Oakland. You never know what you might learn about this other human being. Or what you might learn about yourself. Our ability to sit with each other in that space, through our differences, is the gateway to radical belonging. It is how we learn. It is how we grow. It is how we become.

I hope you'll join me on this journey, good brother and good sister. There's plenty of room on the porch for all of us. The light will always be on, and you're always welcome home.

Acknowledgments

Thank you to my writing team, Elayne Fluker, Peppur Chambers, Bill Cody, Matt Prinz, and Toby Castle, for helping me go from my heart to the pages. Teamwork makes the dream work!

Thank you to my editor, Valerie Weaver-Zercher, who was an early believer in this project and message.

Thank you to Lara Love and the team at Idea Architects for helping bring this book to the public.

Thank you to Dr. john a. powell for your brilliant scholarship and mentorship through this pivotal moment in our world.

Thank you to the Empower Initiative team, who works tirelessly to create a world where everyone belongs.

Thank you to the McBride clan. We don't die; we multiply!

And deep gratitude to all the West Oakland grandmothers, loved ones in East Oakland, young people of Ferguson, mothers in San Francisco and Sacramento: I've been blessed to come alongside you in the struggle for justice. Our labor is not in vain.

Notes

Introduction

One 2019 study: Nathan Kalmoe and Liliana Mason, "Lethal Mass Partisanship: Prevalence, Correlates, and Electoral Contingencies," NCAPSA American Politics Meeting, January 2019, https://www
.dannyhayes.org/uploads/6/9/8/5/69858539/kalmoe___mason
_ncapsa_2019_-_lethal_partisanship_-_final_lmedit.pdf.

Chapter 1

"a set of common processes": See john a. powell and Stephen Menendian, "The Problem of Othering: Towards Inclusiveness and Belonging," Othering & Belonging, 2016, http://www.otheringand
belonging.org/the-problem-of-othering/.

"What you see and hear": C. S. Lewis, *The Magician's Nephew* (New York: HarperCollins, 1955), xx.

Chapter 2

"If I do not stop": Martin Luther King Jr., "On Being a Good Neighbor," sermon, July 1, 1962, https://kinginstitute.stanford.edu/king-papers/documents/draft-chapter-iii-being-good-neighbor.

Chapter 3

"All the great movements": bell hooks, *All about Love: New Visions* (New York: William Morrow, 2018), xix.

"The otherness and threat": john a. powell, "Only Bridging Can Heal a World of Breaking," *Yes!*, November 11, 2019, https://www.yesmagazine.org/issue/building-bridges/2019/11/11/only-bridging-can-heal-a-world-of-breaking.

"We cannot afford to be color blind": See Mellody Hobson, "Color Blind or Color Brave?" TED Talk, March 2014, https://www.youtube.com/watch?v=oKtALHe3Y9Q.

"The most challenging thing": bell hooks, panel conversation, Othering & Belonging Conference, April 26, 2015, https://www.youtube.com/watch?v=0sX7fqIU4gQ.

Dr. Crenshaw called this notion: For more on intersectionality, see Kimberlé Crenshaw, "Demarginalizing the Intersection of Race and Sex: A Black Feminist Critique of Antidiscrimination Doctrine, Feminist Theory, and Antiracist Politics," *University of Chicago Law Forum* 1989 (1989): 1, https://chicagounbound.uchicago.edu/uclf/vol1989/iss1/8/?utm_source=chicagounbound.uchicago.edu%2Fuclf%2Fvol1989%2Fiss1%2F8&utm_medium=PDF&utm_campaign=PDFCoverPages.

Jabari shared his origin story: Jabari Holder, "Pookie and the Pastor," October 16, 2022, on *An Invitation to Become*, produced by Ben McBride, https://empowerinitiative.podbean.com/.

Chapter 4

"the beliefs and the feelings": Jennifer Eberhardt, *Biased: Uncovering the Hidden Prejudice That Shapes What We See, Think and Do* (New York: Viking, 2019), 31.

"The brain needs to sort": Eberhardt, interview by Belinda Luscombe, "What Police Departments and the Rest of Us Can Do to Overcome

Implicit Bias, According to Experts," *TIME*, March 27, 2019, https://
time.com/5558181/jennifer-eberhardt-overcoming-implicit-bias/.

In 2008, I decided: Anastasia Hendricks, "Life in the Killing Zone/
Violence Is the Most Pervasive Part of Growing Up in East Oakland," *San Francisco Chronicle,* February 2, 2003, https://www
.sfgate.com/bayarea/article/Life-in-the-killing-zone-Violence-is
-the-most-2637012.php.

At this last stop in California: To read more about this era, see Isabel
Wilkerson, *The Warmth of Other Suns: The Epic Story of America's
Great Migration* (New York: Vintage, 2011).

The 1950s brought an intensified racial divide: For more on racist housing policies and other issues in this paragraph, see Ta-
Nehisi Coates's "The Case for Reparations," *Atlantic,* June 2014,
https://www.theatlantic.com/magazine/archive/2014/06/the-case
-for-reparations/361631/.

"A suicide note": James Queally, "Accuser in Oakland Police Sex Abuse
Scandal Settles Claim for Nearly $1 Million," *Baltimore Sun*, May
31, 2017, https://www.baltimoresun.com/la-me-ln-oakland-sex
-scandal-settlement-20170531-story.html.

In 2017, the city settled: Brooks Jarosz, "Newly Released Internal Probe
Shows Oakland Officers' Interactions with Teen Girl Used for Sex,"
June 27, 2019, https://www.ktvu.com/news/newly-released-internal
-probe-shows-oakland-officers-interactions-with-teen-girl-used
-for-sex. See also Queally, "Accuser in Oakland."

Chapter 5

After our first year of building: "A Case Study in Hope: Lessons from
Oakland's Remarkable Reduction in Gun Violence," Giffords Law
Center to Prevent Gun Violence, April 23, 2019, https://giffords
.org/lawcenter/report/a-case-study-in-hope-lessons-from-oak
lands-remarkable-reduction-in-gun-violence/.

"live our way into new ways of thinking": This quote has been at-
tributed to various sources.

"the substance of things hoped for": Hebrews 11:1, King James Version.

"Each of us, helplessly and forever": James Baldwin, "Here Be Dragons,"
The Price of the Ticket: Collected Nonfiction, 1948–1985, reprint ed.
(Boston: Beacon Press, 2021), 687.

Chapter 6

We marched down Broadway: Read more about Bring the HEAT at bringtheheat.info.

We went to Washington, DC: To find out more about the history and doctrine and effects of qualified immunity, see Equal Justice Initiative's webpage: https://eji.org/issues/qualified-immunity/.

Black people were still being killed: See "Operation Ghetto Storm," Prison Policy, accessed November 29, 2022, https://www.prison policy.org/scans/Operation-Ghetto-Storm.pdf; Curtis Bunn, "Report: Black People Are Still Killed by Police at a Higher Rate Than Other Groups," NBC News, March 3, 2022, https://www .nbcnews.com/news/nbcblk/report-black-people-arc-still-killed -police-higher-rate-groups-rcna17169; and www.mappingpolice violence.org.

I realized we were losing our ability: To find out more, see Chimamanda Ngozi Adichie's TED Talk: https://www.ted.com/talks /chimamanda_ngozi_adichie_the_danger_of_a_single_story?lan guage=en.

"What if this darkness": Valarie Kaur, *See No Stranger: A Memoir and Manifesto of Revolutionary Love* (New York: One World, 2021), xi.

"There is nothing in all the world": Martin Luther King Jr., "A Creative Protest," February 16, 1960, https://kinginstitute.stanford.edu /king-papers/documents/creative-protest#:~:text=Victor%20Hugo %20once%20said%20that,the%20iron%20feet%20of%20 oppression.

"Power concedes nothing": Frederick Douglass, "West India Emancipation Speech," August 3, 1857, https://rbscp.lib.rochester.edu /4398.

Even science says: Jill Suttie and Jason Marsh, "Five Ways Giving Is Good for You," *Greater Good Magazine*, December 13, 2010, https://greater good.berkeley.edu/article/item/5_ways_giving_is_good_for_you.

Chapter 7

"Resting as a form of resistance": Tricia Hersey, *Rest Is Resistance: A Manifesto* (New York: Little Brown Spark, 2022), 16.

Chapter 8

"Power without love": Martin Luther King Jr., *Where Do We Go from Here: Chaos or Community?* Illustrated ed. (Boston: Beacon Press, 2010), 38.